Friends in Faith

Mentoring Youth In the Church

CHARLES KISHPAUGH

BARBARA BRUCE

DISCIPLESHIP RESOURCES

MATERIALS FOR GROWTH IN CHRISTIAN FAITH & LIFE

NASHVILLE, TENNESSEE

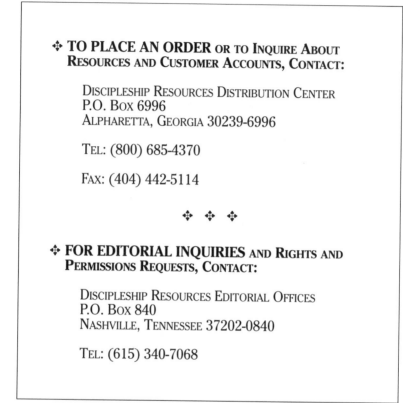

❖ **TO PLACE AN ORDER** OR TO INQUIRE ABOUT RESOURCES AND CUSTOMER ACCOUNTS, CONTACT:

DISCIPLESHIP RESOURCES DISTRIBUTION CENTER
P.O. BOX 6996
ALPHARETTA, GEORGIA 30239-6996

TEL: (800) 685-4370

FAX: (404) 442-5114

❖ ❖ ❖

❖ **FOR EDITORIAL INQUIRIES** AND RIGHTS AND PERMISSIONS REQUESTS, CONTACT:

DISCIPLESHIP RESOURCES EDITORIAL OFFICES
P.O. BOX 840
NASHVILLE, TENNESSEE 37202-0840

TEL: (615) 340-7068

Cover design by Ann L. Cummings.

Unless otherwise noted, all scripture quotations are from the New Revised Standard Version of the Holy Bible, copyright © 1989 by the Division of Christian Education of the National Council of the Churches of Christ in the United States of America. Used by permission.

Library of Congress Card Catalog No. 93-73443

ISBN 0-88177-128-7

DR128

Contents

1 MODELS

IN THE SPRING, along the Natchez Trace Parkway in Tennessee, one can witness a strange sight: turtles trying to cross the road. The turtles try; but as they try, some of them become confused by the passing cars and trucks and turn back. Others forge ahead. A few make it across to the other side — either by luck or by the skill of the drivers of the vehicles. Many are run over. Pondering this scene, one could wish that the turtles had a guide to lead them.

In a similar vein, in Lewis Carroll's *Alice's Adventures in Wonderland*, Alice asks for guidance from the Cheshire Cat.

"Would you tell me, please, which way I ought to go from here?"

"That depends a good deal on where you want to get to," said the Cat.

"I don't much care where —" said Alice.

"Then it doesn't matter which way you go," said the Cat.

"— so long as I get somewhere," Alice added as an explanation.

"Oh, you're sure to do that," said the Cat, "if you only walk long enough."[1]

Like the turtles in Tennessee, and Alice in Wonderland, youth today are on a journey and need guidance. Some youth start their journey well, then get distracted, turn back, and lose their way. Others simply have no direction and are not sure they even need one. Just as surely as the turtles and Alice, however, youth need guidance from someone who has already faced and made it through some of the dangers, someone who knows the way (or at least part of it), someone who understands how important it is to have a destination. This is where the role of the adult mentor begins.

A BASIC DEFINITION

The term *mentor* comes down to us in the story of Ulysses from Homer's *Odyssey*.[2] When Ulysses left home on his journeys, he left his

1

son, Telemachus, with a person who would watch over him, provide for his schooling, and be a companion. The man's name was Mentor. The distinction between the role of parent and that of mentor is important (see the discussion of the "benefits" of mentoring, pages 11-25). For now, however, we need to begin with a simple definition of mentoring in the context of faith.

In general, mentoring is a time to engage another person in a dialogue of faith. For our purposes, in relation to youth ministry in the church, we shall define mentoring as *a time for a caring and spiritually mature adult to engage a youth in a dialogue of faith*. This definition implies many things; but most of all, it implies that mentoring in faith is a *pilgrimage*.

By definition, a pilgrimage is a journey, implying movement and growth. Those who enter into this journey must be open to changes in themselves, their faith, and their direction in life. They need to recognize that God moves in many ways to bring faith to life. This is true both for the adult and for the youth. In this light, the role of the adult is not to indoctrinate the young person into the beliefs of the church, but to be a partner with God, enabling faith to come to the surface and to take form. Thus, mentoring is not a time of judgment, but a time to explore, wrestle with, and pray about faith issues. It is a time to discover a relationship with God, to make a commitment to God, to seek God's will, and to explore the doubts and assurances of living in faith.

On the journey of mentoring, adults and youth are called to be partners. God calls an adult with much life experience to walk on a quest of faith with a younger person with less life experience. Jesus praised children and said that we must become like them in order to enter the kingdom of heaven. Jesus also had great respect for the tradition and wisdom of the elders. He drew upon their wisdom and example in his own ministry. Both adults and youth have unique gifts to bring to this shared journey. As faith partners, both the adult and the young person commit themselves to be with each other on the journey. In a sense, each is to be a mentor to the other. Each will learn from and spur growth in the other as they make the faith journey together.

All of this implies that mentoring is not an end in itself, but a way of giving and gaining strength in a common journey. Growing in faith is a lifelong experience. At their best, mentor relationships enable each partner to broaden her or his experience of God acting in the world. The partners will never forget their relationship. Like Jesus and the men and women closest to him, a mentoring partnership may well provide deep and long-lasting friendships for life.

Mentoring can be one of the most powerful experiences in a person's life. It thrives when people earnestly search with one another and make time to commit to the process. It falls short, however, when persons do not take it seriously, or try to fit it into "leftover" time in their lives.

HISTORICAL MODELS

History contains many models of mentoring related to the professions. These can be instructive for mentoring in the church as well. In previous centuries, for example, the only way to learn a trade or profession was to attach oneself as an apprentice to someone who had already mastered the craft. In Jesus' time, carpenters and other workers did not go to school as we know it. They attached themselves to a mentor.

The apprentice system provided a good means to train the early artisan. The skilled carpenter knew the nature and properties of different kinds of woods, and the best ways to cut the wood to obtain maximum strength and beauty. The carpenter's muscles knew just how to shape, bend, or fit the wood. All of this took years of learning and practice. Apprenticeship also had an economic motive. An apprentice could not make a living competing against the experienced carpenter. So the apprentice agreed to do menial labor in return for the carpenter's help in learning the skills needed to become a proven carpenter.

The one-room school is another historic example of mentoring. In the earlier decades of this century in the United States, towns and municipalities often did not have enough money to provide school buildings with numerous rooms for a variety of teachers. As a result, several classes often had to meet together in one room with one teacher. Under such conditions, it was impossible for the teacher to teach lessons to all of the age groups at the same time. Therefore, the teacher would choose older students as mentors for the younger ones. The older students prepared the lessons, taught the younger students, and sometimes administered tests. The older students discovered much that they had not learned or remembered when they were younger. To be a mentor is to reinforce more deeply what one learned the first time.

Recent studies have argued that the one-room school may have been one of the most effective teaching and learning arrangements ever practiced in this country. Some educators have even suggested returning to some of the strengths of this model, including the idea of using older students to teach the younger.

Likewise, the medical profession uses a form of mentoring in its residency requirements. In the final stages of their training, after they have completed their academic studies, medical students spend time in the residency program of a hospital or clinic. During the period of residency, the new doctors learn from other more experienced doctors. They follow the experienced doctors around on visits from hospital room to hospital room, listening at first, then making their own simple diagnoses under supervision.

We might add many more examples of mentoring in a variety of other professions — law, agriculture, business, and others. The point, however, is not to pile up examples but to recognize the importance of mentoring in the process of handing skills from one generation to the next.

BIBLICAL MODELS

The Bible also contains images and stories of mentoring. Not all of these are positive in every respect. The story of Eli and Samuel, for example, shows that Samuel turned out well despite some very poor mentoring on the part of Eli. Among the most positive stories, however, three are outstanding: Naomi and Ruth, Jesus and Peter, Paul and Timothy.

According to the book of Ruth in the Old Testament, Naomi and her husband, Elimelech, had two sons who moved with them to the land of Moab because of famine in Israel. Ruth, a native daughter of Moab, married one of Naomi's sons. Naomi's husband and sons later died, and Naomi decided to leave Moab in order to return to her ancestral home. When Naomi spoke of her plan to leave, Ruth responded with a brief yet poignant speech that has ever since been regarded as a model of loyalty:

> *Do not press me to leave you or to turn back from following you!*
> *Where you go, I will go; where you lodge, I will lodge; your people*
> *shall be my people, and your God my God. Where you die, I will*
> *die — there will I be buried (Ruth 1:16-17).*

Ruth had already learned much from Naomi, and she wanted to continue learning. She wanted to be of the people Naomi represented. She wanted to be with Naomi in mind, body, and soul.

When they returned to Israel, Ruth continued to look to Naomi as a mentor. She sought advice about where to gather food and how to behave. She also followed Naomi's instruction in matters of the heart, eventually getting married again to a good man named Boaz. Though we could wish for more details about the relationship between Ruth and Naomi, one thing is perfectly clear — Ruth saw something of value in Naomi that she wanted to emulate. That is why Ruth chose Naomi as her mentor.

We find other biblical images of mentoring in both the Old and the New Testaments. According to the Gospel of Luke, for example, Jesus was walking by the Sea of Galilee one day when he encountered two fishermen who were having no success with their nets (Luke 5:1-11). Thus began one of the most turbulent and interesting mentoring relationships in the entire Bible — that of Jesus and Peter.

The relationship between Jesus and Peter was full of good times and hard times. Just consider a few of the highlights (and low points) of their story. When Jesus first called him, Peter immediately left his nets to follow (Mark 1:16-18). One day on a stormy sea, Peter asked Jesus to help him walk on the water, later sinking in unbelief (Matthew 14:28-31). Peter was always impulsive. When Jesus knelt to wash the disciples' feet, Peter refused, until Jesus made this act a condition of their friendship; then Peter asked to be washed all over (John 13:1-9). On another occasion, Peter boldly identified Jesus as the promised Messiah (Mark 8:27-29). And in one of the most poignant sequences in all of scripture, Peter first promised to follow Jesus to the death, then denied and abandoned him, finally embracing a ministry that would lead to his own death (Mark 14:26-31, 66-72; and John 21:15-19). Tradition says that Peter was crucified at Rome — upside down, because he felt unworthy to die in the same position as his Master.

Throughout their time together, Jesus taught Peter by word and deed, by precept and example. Jesus spoke words of encouragement to Peter — as when he declared Peter's faith to be a benchmark for the church (Matthew 16:13-19). But Jesus also challenged Peter to rise above self-serving attitudes—as when he led Peter and two other disciples away from comfortable seclusion on the Mount of Transfiguration in order to return with them to ministry in the valley and in the city (Luke 9:28-38). Though Jesus clearly took initiative in the relationship, he also made himself available to Peter for questions. He did not ask if Peter had any questions, but his attitude of openness made Peter feel confident to ask questions. Jesus' answers were sometimes gentle and at other times firm and forceful.

Through it all, Jesus gave Peter time and space in which to grow, to learn, and to change. He knew that Peter would only come to understand things gradually; yet he believed that Peter would eventually come to understand. Nowhere was this clearer than in the sequence of events that led through Peter's denial to his eventual martyrdom. In all of this Jesus showed how a good mentor allows the partner to struggle, even to fail, in order to work things through over time in a way that brings real change and growth.

The examples of Naomi and Ruth, and Jesus and Peter, show much about the biblical model of mentoring. But now let's move to one more biblical example, the relationship of Paul and Timothy.

According to the New Testament record, Paul accepted Timothy as a companion and friend. In the early part of the relationship, the church had commissioned Paul to travel to various places in order to spread the good news about Jesus and the kingdom of God. Paul sent for Timothy to accompany him on these journeys. It was during these times that Timothy experienced Paul's love and devotion to Jesus. If we examine the relationship between Paul and Timothy closely, we can discern at least five basic principles that characterize effective mentoring relationships.

First, a mentor trusts his/her friend in faith to do things without supervision. Paul sent Timothy out to do things on his own, testing his skills and his faith, learning by doing (Acts 19:22; 1 Corinthians 4:17). Learning takes place best when the teacher enables the student to be in ministry. This is true in relation to Sunday school teachers as well. Often the students learn the lesson best when they are allowed to be involved in teaching it. (Remember the one-room schoolhouse?)

Second, the mentor protects the friend in faith from that which he or she cannot handle, helping to ensure that the friend in faith has a positive experience. Paul certainly saw it as part of his responsibility to protect Timothy in this way. In 1 Corinthians 16:10-11 Paul urged the members of the Church at Corinth:

> *If Timothy comes, see that he has nothing to fear among you, for he is doing the work of the Lord just as I am; therefore let no one despise him. Send him on his way in peace, so that he may come to me; for I am expecting him with the brothers.*

Mentors provide a degree of safety for their disciples. The mentor does not take away all risk, for it is through risk that we learn; but mentors stand with us in risk and give us strength and support.

Third, the mentor treats the friend in faith as an equal, without condescending or criticizing. Paul included Timothy as an equal in their communications with the churches (2 Corinthians 1:1; Philippians 1:1; Colossians 1:1; 1 Thessalonians 1:1). This not only paved the way for many to receive Timothy — because Paul had marked him as someone important — it also gave Timothy an important basis for strengthening self-esteem. An effective mentor will build up his or her disciple in the presence of others whenever possible.

Fourth, when circumstances require, an effective mentor can be firm in challenging the friend in faith. When Paul closed his first letter to Timothy, he offered some personal, perhaps corrective, instruction:

Timothy, guard what has been entrusted to you. Avoid the profane chatter and contradictions of what is falsely called knowledge; by professing it some have missed the mark as regards the faith.

The mentor can be firm and call her or his disciples to live up to an expected standard. An effective mentor will not resort to casuistry — that is, trying to create a code of correct behavior for every situation. Rather, the mentor will help the friend in faith learn how to discern the guidance of the Spirit and, thus, avoid behaviors not in keeping with the Spirit of Christ.

Fifth, the mentor offers the friend in faith continual encouragement and support. Paul offered Timothy such encouragement on many occasions. In 1 Timothy 1:18-19, Paul couched his instructions for Timothy in a tone that was unmistakably generous, hopeful, and confident of the best:

I am giving you these instructions, Timothy, my child, in accordance with the prophecies made earlier about you, so that by following them you may fight the good fight, having faith and a good conscience.

A mentor helps his or her disciples walk boldly in life. Paul not only offered Timothy practical guidelines and instructions, he also made it clear that Timothy could depend on his genuine friendship and affection.

ECCLESIAL MODELS

The tradition of the church through the ages also contains significant examples of mentoring. In the ancient church, during the monastic period, Christians practiced gentle confrontation, discussed problems, and helped one another know the presence of God in daily life. Spiritual leaders often went into the wilderness to seek a closer relationship with God. They were known for wisdom and holiness. When others became disillusioned with life, they sought out these spiritual guides in order to ask their deepest questions, share their doubts, and seek peace.

Following the example of antiquity, the church of the Middle Ages in Ireland developed the tradition of the "soul friend." Edward C. Sellner tells the story of the Irish soul friend in his book, *Mentoring*.[3] The soul friend, or *anamchara*, is a spiritual tutor or mentor to a seeking person. The two persons spend much time together talking about their visions, lives, and examples of a spiritual life. The soul friend is mature and compassionate; respects others and keeps confidences. The soul friend is one who knows how to disclose self and discern the movements of the spirit in the heart.[4] The soul friend is a prototype of the model of mentoring that is presented in this book.

The commitment to mentoring is not, however, only an ancient phenomenon. In the order of worship of many churches today, we find a fresh statement of commitment to those practices of nurture and sustenance that are the essence of mentoring. For example, when a baby or a child is baptized in The United Methodist Church, the pastor asks the congregation to respond to the following question:

> *Members of the household of faith,*
> *I commend to your love and care this child,*
>   *whom we this day recognize as a member of the family of God.*
> *Will you endeavor so to live*
>   *that this child may grow in the knowledge and love of God,*
>   *through our Savior Jesus Christ?*

The people respond:

> *With God's help*
> *we will so order our lives after the example of Christ,*
> *that this child, surrounded by steadfast love,*
> *may be established in the faith,*
> *and confirmed and strengthened*
> *in the way that leads to life eternal.*[5]

In another place the pastor asks the people:

> *Do you as a congregation*
> *accept the responsibility of assisting these parents*
>   *in fulfillment of the baptismal vows,*
> *and do you undertake to provide facilities and opportunities*
>   *for Christian nurture and fellowship?*

The people respond:

> *We will, by the grace of God.*[6]

To be sure, not all Christian denominations believe in or practice infant baptism. Nevertheless, the church through the ages has always recognized its calling to nurture faith in the next generation. The United Methodist ritual simply expresses this commitment in the context of infant baptism. The members of the congregation affirm their commitment to assist parents in providing faithful nurture and support for each child. They recognize that this is only possible by the continuing presence and supply of God's grace. In a word, they welcome the child into the journey of faith which they themselves continue to travel. These vows express the very essence of a commitment to mentoring. (See also the discussion of mentoring in the context of confirmation on pages 27-28.)

A CONTEMPORARY MODEL

We have been exploring a variety of models — historical, scriptural, and ecclesial — that show what a mentoring ministry might look like. Now let's look at mentoring in a slightly different way by describing the actual experience of a contemporary congregation.

Picture a group of youth and adults sitting in the parlor of their church evaluating the Christian mentoring program that they started the year before. The program paired a youth and an adult in the church for a three-month period. The purpose was to explore issues of faith and life. They knew of other congregations who were involved in mentoring programs, but this was their first try at such a program.

Jack spoke of his experience first, noting that he had been almost ready to leave the church. Because of school and Saturday sports, Sunday was the only day he could sleep in. He explained that Sunday school and worship bored him. He still believed in God, Christ, and heaven, but he did not think he needed church to help with that. About that time he joined the mentoring program in the church. He hadn't really wanted to join, but his mother had insisted, because this was part of joining the church.

Jack's mentor, Henry, said that he too had become complacent in his Christianity. Much of his religious activity was routine. He found value in certain traditions from the past, and he continued to come to church; but most of what he did, he did solely out of habit. He was much too busy with work and family to give time to a new Christian activity. Christianity was still important to him, but it was more a background activity than a significant element in his life. He wanted to spend time at a renewal center to discover what was missing, but he could not find the time in his busy schedule. At that point in his life, Henry was asked to be Jack's mentor. Henry had not seen the invitation as a time to strengthen his own faith, but it had become that as he met with Jack.

Jack recalled their first meeting. They were both very nervous and unsure of what to say. Jack did not talk much to adults, other than to his parents and teachers. Henry had even less occasion to talk to youth. His two daughters were grown and had their own homes. Jack and Henry started talking about sports because they each thought the other might be interested—and because they did not know what else to talk about. As they met more frequently, the conversation dipped into more important areas of life. They talked about their faith, about how important God was in their lives, and about some of their doubts and concerns. They talked about times they felt closest to God. Finally, Jack revealed his boredom at worship and in Sunday school; he confided that he had been strongly considering not coming any more.

Henry then told Jack of his concerns about his own Christianity. To tackle their mutual problem of boredom at church, Jack and Henry started discussing Sunday's scripture and the sermon for a portion of their time each week. They also joined a team from the church that winterized houses for homebound persons in the community. They both felt more involved in the church and more alive in the worship sessions. They no longer talked of sleeping in on Sunday.

Having found common ground, Henry and Jack talked about Christianity's importance in all of life — at work, at school, at play, with family, and with others. They discussed how their faith was important in making decisions about money, relationships, sex, drugs, honesty, and other real-life issues. They talked a lot about everything. Henry and Jack became good friends and enjoyed their time together. These events, and Jack and Henry's growing friendship, kept them meeting long after the three months had passed. For Jack and Henry, mentoring became not so much a program as a way of life — a way of sharing and growing in faith and life.

2 | BENEFITS

YOUTH AND ADULTS BENEFIT GREATLY when they are able to enter into a dialogue of faith. We need such dialogue today as never before in the history of our culture. According to H. Stephen Glenn, contemporary society tends to isolate youth from adults in nearly every setting — at school, at church, in social settings, and even at home.[7] By contrast, a well-organized mentoring program brings youth and adults back together in significant dialogue — that is, if adults and youth are willing to take the time to let it work. Moreover, the benefits of mentoring extend not only to youth, but also to adults, to the congregation as a whole, and to the wider society.

SELF-ESTEEM

One of the greatest challenges young people face is the challenge of developing healthy self-esteem. Many youth today simply do not feel that they are capable or competent at anything. Our society encourages a great deal of competition among youth. Young people are asked to compare themselves with each other, with siblings, and with adults. Competition can be healthy, of course; but it can also be destructive when a young person feels that his or her value is entirely dependent on winning or succeeding in a particular activity or on a particular occasion. Few things can more effectively keep these matters in proper perspective than an open and caring relationship with a spiritually mature adult.

Though there are no published studies that measure the exact effect of mentoring on the self-esteem of youth, the effect is nonetheless undeniable. Consider, for example, the story of Sandra. Sandra was often down on herself. One might say that she was her own worst critic. She believed she was not very smart or attractive; she thought people did not like her and did not want to hear what she had to say. She made life miserable for herself. In reality, people just thought she was shy; as a result, they let her withdraw in social settings, allowing her to behave in

11

ways that further separated her from others. No one tried to help her be more assertive. As a result, Sandra's low self-esteem was only reinforced.

Then Sandra joined the mentoring program at her church and was paired with an adult whom she chose. The adult listened to her, treated her ideas as important, and helped her learn to be happy with her appearance. This did not happen overnight. Indeed, it took several months. But as Sandra and her mentor talked over faith and life issues, she slowly began to believe in her own ideas and opinions. She also showed improvement at school and at home by becoming more outgoing and unafraid of expressing her opinions.

Sandra's story reminds us that we are all on a pilgrimage. We try to realize God's purpose for our lives; we look for our place in the world, but we often get discouraged or distracted. We all need the support of others in order to keep our focus and courage. This is especially true for youth. With the help of a caring adult, a young person can interact with the world in effective ways and learn to discern God's purpose in her or his life. One study registered the following results when youth met with pastors in a truly supportive environment.

> For two separate evenings, the pastors sat and actively listened to these youth share their concerns (and later their evaluations of how well the pastors listened). We were impressed by the fact that many friendships were formed between the pastors and youth, friendships that often continued through the year via letters. When several youths were queried about these friendships, one said, "You don't understand. Never before in my life have I had an adult listen to me for forty-five minutes. It's a good experience."[8]

A stable and caring mentoring relationship can help youth build healthy self-esteem, and this finally touches every area of a young person's life. One writer put it this way: "More than anything else, the attainment of a healthy sense of identity and a feeling of self-esteem gives young people a perspective, a way of looking at themselves and others, which enables them to manage the majority of stress situations."[9]

CONFIDENCES

Closely related to the power of self-esteem in youth is the value of sharing confidence in relationship with others. If self-esteem has to do with how one values oneself, confidence has to do with trusting others and feeling valuable to them. In this area too, a mentoring relationship between a youth and an adult can have remarkable results.

By the very nature of their age and station in life, youth are dealing with a lot of confusing changes. Their bodies are changing. Their relationships to parents and family are changing. As Arthur Jersild has pointed out, such changes are a natural part of growing up: "Ideas and attitudes pertaining to the self have been evolving since earliest childhood. They show considerable stability before a person reaches adolescent years, but much happens in the course of adolescence that makes it necessary for adolescents to take a fresh look at themselves."[10] Going through such changes is natural; but it is not easy. Youth need someone to talk to, someone who can be trusted, someone in whom to *confide*.

Oftentimes youth turn to their peers. Most youth have many questions and are exploring a variety of answers to them. Youth learn much from their peers. Some information is helpful and moves them forward in their journey; but much of peer learning can be a downward path. More to our immediate point, young people know very well that they cannot always trust each other to keep confidences that have been shared. Youthful friendships can be fickle, and few things hurt more than the betrayal of a personal secret. This may sound critical of the peer relationship, but experience has shown what many youth already sense: They need someone in addition to their peers in order to strengthen their sense of confidence.

To varying degrees, youth also confide in their parents. This, however, is not an answer for everything. After all, part of what youth are trying to figure out and work through is how their relationship to parents is changing. Do I agree with my parents about everything? Am I supposed to? Do I have to tell my parents everything? Should I feel guilty if I don't? Where am I free to be different and to have my own personal thoughts? Youth often need someone in addition to parents in order to talk openly and candidly about such questions — someone who will listen, someone who can be trusted to keep confidences once they are shared.

This again is where the role of an adult mentor has great potential. Mentoring relationships provide a place where it is more than just OK to talk about personal questions of faith and life: It is positively encouraged. Indeed, this is the focus of the time that mentoring partners spend together. A youth can often ask important questions of an adult that he or she would hesitate to ask either of a peer or of a parent. These questions may deal with personal faith, doubts, sexual changes, other people's reactions, hopes for the future, and fears about the future. The mentor listens confidentially nonjudgmentally. The mentor supports, questions, and leads. The mentor talks about his or her own faith in honest, forthright ways. The mentor provides an atmosphere in which it is safe to explore and to grow in faith.

Consider the story of one youth who was very concerned about some dreams he was having. His dreams were filled with sexual images. He awoke very excited, but with mixed emotions about the images. He was interested in the dreams, but he also felt guilty about them. His experiences at school and at church left him unsure whether to consider the dreams normal or to think of them as "dirty" or evil in some way. He was confused and began to withdraw from conversation in youth group. He lacked the courage to talk with his parents, because he did not think they would understand. Sex and sexual thoughts were not openly discussed in his home. Likewise, he was sure his friends would laugh at him, and he never had a chance to talk privately to his sex education teacher at school. In the mentoring program of his church, however, this young man found a place where he could gradually open up about his feelings and sort through his fears and confusion.

In many ways, the world is not a safe place. Youth know few persons who can be trusted to listen to them without repeating the information shared or taking advantage of the situation. With an adult mentor, however, a youth can share real concerns with the confidence of being heard and respected. The mentor is a safe person with whom the youth can explore and see that others have walked the path before. This is a time for the youth to confide in another trustworthy person, to trust and be trusted, and thus to build confidence in relationship with others. (See also the discussion of child abuse issues on pages 40-41.)

SUPPORT FOR PARENTS

We have already mentioned at several points how youth struggle with growing up in relation to their parents. Anyone who is or has been a parent to a teenager, however, knows that growing up can be a struggle for parents as well. Most parents are concerned about the needs of youth — about the processes that youth go through in growing up physically, emotionally, and spiritually; but many parents find it difficult to translate their concern into effective communication and action.

For parents, the adolescent years are fraught with conflict, mis-understanding, and a search by both youth and parents to define new roles. Youth are at a confusing and tumultuous stage of development. They test themselves and nearly everyone around them. Their values may often appear to be based solely on the latest fad or on what the members of the "in" group are doing, wearing, or saying. What parent has not argued with a teenaged youth over a particular style or name brand of clothing? These desires for the right clothes may often seem more driving than the desire to be honest or caring.

To make matters worse, today's parents often feel they are not equipped to guide the spiritual and moral formation of their young. The Search Institute report on the Sunday school indicates that youth who come from families that discuss their Christian faith are more likely to have a mature faith than those from families that do not discuss their faith. The study also shows, however, that most parents do not discuss faith issues as much as their youth desire. Several factors affect this phenomenon.

For one thing, individuals in most families today are quite busy. Many families spend almost no time sitting down to talk about anything. Often, discussion time between parents and youth is in automobiles with younger or older siblings present and with considerable distraction from traffic. Discussions involving spiritual matters require time to get started and time to complete; but time is one of the least available commodities in the modern family relationship.

Scarcity of time is itself part of a larger historical phenomenon: the breakdown of the extended family since at least the 1950s. During the time leading up to World War II, youth were raised by several adults: their parents, grandparents, aunts, and uncles. These persons all lived in the same community and sometimes in the same house as the youth. There was a whole cadre of adults youth could to look for guidance and support. As one writer has commented, "Relatives can add a wonderful extra dimension to any child's life. In fact, sometimes children feel closer to a cousin than to their brother or sister, closer to an aunt than to their own mother. They may tell secrets to a grandparent that they would never tell anyone else in the world."[11] During the Fifties, however, families began to experience the results of greater mobility. Parents often moved with their children to a different city or town. The extended family came together less and less. As a consequence, children and youth interacted less with other adults, and youth often began to seek an extended family among their peers.

Moreover, parents of today's youth are of a generation that often lacks religious experience in community. When these parents were youth, they took up issues such as justice and freedom, but their focus was often on *individual* freedom of spirituality and expression. For several generations now, people have had the impression that they must grow up on their own, that there is no one to help: "Clearly, {today} the meaning of one's life for most Americans is to become one's own person, almost to give birth to oneself. Much of this process is negative. It involves breaking from family, community, and inherited ideas."[12] As a result, many parents find that they are at the same level in community spiritual awareness (including the stories of the church) as their children. They struggle along with their children, asking the same questions. Many are embarrassed at their level of spirituality and do not know how to discuss faith issues with their children. These parents send their youth to church hoping they will learn something about faith there.

Parents need something or someone to help fill the vacuum in their own lives and in the lives of their families created by the absence of other significant adults. Urie Bronfenbrenner in *Two Worlds of Children* describes the seriousness of the situation:

> It is our view that the phenomenon of segregation by age and its consequences for human behavior and development pose problems of the greatest magnitude for the Western world in general and for American society in particular. As we read the evidence, both from our own research and that of others, we cannot escape the conclusion that, if the current trend persists, if the institutions of our society continue to remove parents, other adults, and older youth from active participation in the lives of children, and if the resulting vacuum is filled by the age-segregated peer group, we can anticipate increased alienation, indifference, antagonism, and violence on the part of the younger generation.[13]

All of this shows how important it is for parents to have the support of other spiritually mature adults to help with the nurture of their youth. For one thing, parents need other trustworthy adults to help their youth learn how to develop relationships with adults. Building adult relationships does not just happen; youth need to learn acceptable behavior and expectations in dealing with other adults. Youth need the experience of growing into new relationships and practicing modes of behavior. A mentor provides an opportunity for youth to experience adult relationships much as youth did in years past.

Likewise, mentors can sometimes help alleviate pressure from tension-filled situations that result from a lack of communication. They can provide a sounding board for youth to speak their minds on issues they perceive as conflict and no-win situations at home. Sometimes just the opportunity to talk with another adult removes a great deal of the pressure that seems to build in families with adolescents. A mentor can often listen more objectively in a non-parental mindset and thus better hear the youth's side of issues. Indeed, on some occasions, the mentor may even be able to help in moderating a conflict between parent and youth.

If the mentor is willing, he or she might be able to throw a new light on the parenting role. The mentor may present the parent's primary concern as care for the youth's well-being, not as policing, preaching, or lecturing — which is what youth often perceive. Mentors can help youth understand the reasons behind the parent's actions. For example, youth often view their parents' ideas about religion with some degree of doubt. They may feel that faith is a "should," something that parents enforce. When a youth can deal with other adults who live out faith and talk about faith issues because they want to, faith takes on new meanings. The mentor does not enforce religion. Rather, the mentor presents faith because it is something important in life. This, in turn, may help youth gain new insight and respect for their parents' faith and values.

The flip side of this issue, of course, is that the parents hear about their youth from someone with an objectivity that they may lack. (This does not mean that mentors violate the confidentiality of the relationship.) Parents may gain new insights into their daughters or sons as they see mentors viewing their youth as persons of worth and value. Parents' eyes gleam when another adult tells them that their youth do indeed have values and standards and that their teachings have not gone unheeded. Under the different hairstyle, the distinctive clothing, and the slang language hides a youth with manners, values, and qualities of which parents can be proud.

Naturally, none of this should suggest that mentors can replace parents as the primary source of spiritual nurture and guidance in the lives of youth. Throughout history, parental love has been a metaphor for the relationship of God to people. Studies show, moreover, that parents are the primary and most significant influence on the faith and values of their children. Indeed, even parents who cannot articulate their spirituality, their religious life story, or their Christian vocational calling, nonetheless serve as models to their children. Their lives provide a grounding, a sense of what should be. But youth also need to check their parents' values to see if they are valid; and in this process, other adults in the church can provide a significant point of comparison. When youth are encouraged to make these kinds of comparisons, they will often discover new insights and a sense of respect for the spiritual values of their parents.

Consider the story of Sherry and Donna. Sherry selected Donna to be her mentor. Sherry babysat Donna's children, and a good rapport developed between them. In the mentoring situation, Donna and Sherry had lots of long talks about what it is like being a teenager, the hassles of school, thoughts about parents, and the newness of dating. Sherry found Donna easy to talk to. She told Donna things about her friends and family that bothered her and that she had not discussed with another adult, including her parents. Faith issues were a natural outgrowth of these conversations. Christian beliefs related to all of the issues. In addition to determining how they felt, they explored what the Bible says about various issues.

Donna told Sherry's mother how responsible and "grown up" Sherry was in decision making and in dealing with issues that confronted her. Donna also encouraged Sherry to talk with her mother, partly to increase her mother's trust in Sherry's ability to handle problems. As a result, Sherry and her mother were able to talk about Sherry's conscious decision not to get involved with a group of students experimenting with alcohol, because Sherry had first talked about it with Donna. Donna was another significant adult in Sherry's life, one to whom she felt she could talk more openly than to her parents. The relationship proved very meaningful and still continues nearly four years after it began. The two young women talk as adults and laugh over common experiences.

The growth that Donna, Sherry, and Sherry's parents gained from this relationship cannot be measured. A mutual trust and respect that formed from the mentoring program will be a permanent part of the lives of all concerned. In this way, a mentoring program should be seen as a complement to the parents' role. As youth mature, they naturally move away from their families and question some family practices. Mentoring can serve as an important bridge during this period of transition — a bridge connecting the young person to the heritage of family and to the adult world.

FAITH DEVELOPMENT

Along with the benefits to youth and parents, mentoring also strengthens the ministry of the church. The church through the ages has always recognized — at least in theory — an obligation to nurture the faith of the next generation. Having this interest and being able to fulfill it, however, can be two very different things. As children become youth and go through the changes of adolescence, they often leave the church. In other words, just at the point where faith development may be most crucial, the opportunity is often lost. The reasons for this are several.

One of the most significant factors in the departure of youth from the church is their innate need to search and question. Youth have many questions about religion and faith. In today's world, they are constantly confronted with a bewildering array of spiritual alternatives. Through a variety of media (including movies, documentaries, and in-person proselytizing) they are exposed to religious practices and spiritual options their parents and grandparents never dreamed of — from the very conservative Christian to the very liberal, from New Age channeling and crystals to Eastern religions, cults, and even satanism. All of this can be rather heady (and dangerous) stuff for an impressionable teenager — especially one who has come to take for granted the spiritual heritage of his or her own faith tradition.

At the same time, the church cannot simply blame the departure of youth on the influence of other religions. Indeed, another reason youth leave the church has to do with the way the church itself is often organized. Even the most well-intentioned congregations often neglect, overlook, or ignore their youth. In some cases, the church simply does not provide a forum in which youth can candidly raise questions. The typical settings for Christian education—for example, a Sunday school class or a youth group meeting—are important, but they do not always provide the best opportunity for a young person to be transparent about his or her questions and doubts. Often there is little time for indepth personal questions and, even if time is allotted, many youth will be hesitant to share because of peer dynamics (*Whom must I impress? What will the others think?*). The Christian education program of a congregation is necessary to the growth of each youth, but the program needs support and augmentation.

To make matters worse, statistics show that the church has a limited time frame within which to reach youth effectively. The Search Institute of Effective Christian Education, in its study of mainline Protestant denominations, determined that most youth break away from the church when their parents agree to make attendance optional.[14] This typically occurs at one of two points — either after the completion of confirmation or after graduation from high school. If a youth has not discovered something of meaning and value in church by this time, he or she may leave the church with no definite plan to return.

In response to these needs and problems, mentoring can help the church fulfill its commitment to the faith development of youth. A mentoring relationship with a caring and spiritually mature adult provides resources for faith development that youth may not receive in any other way. With the inclusion of another significant adult in the life of a youth, faith issues are presented in an atmosphere of caring, without judgments or lectures. In a mentoring program, youth begin to take an active role side-by-side with the adults of the church. This joint activity promotes dialogue and serves as the basis for beginning to understand one another's views, opinions, and rationale for life behavior. Generations work, learn, and grow together.

In this light, it is difficult to imagine a more effective method for faith development than the relational approach of mentoring. According to George Gallup in *The Religious Life of Young Americans*, mentoring is an important component of the most successful youth programs. Young people of all ages can be mentored "by those who remember what it was like to be young, and who realize that it may be very different to be young today."[15] Likewise, the Search Institute determined that Christian education for youth is most effective when it "emphasizes intergenerational contact" and "creates a sense of community in which people help each other develop their faith and values."[16]

This does not mean that a mentoring program can or should operate independently of other aspects of Christian education. Indeed, as we shall see in the discussion of confirmation (pages 27-28), mentoring can be combined effectively with many of the standard settings of Christian education. Mentoring does, however, add a dimension of personal relationship and individual attention that has often been missing from conventional settings.

CONNECTING FAITH AND LIFE

Closely related to the task of faith development is the creative challenge of connecting faith with everyday life. This is a challenge for all Christians, but it is especially a challenge for youth. Youth stand at the beginning of their adult lives, with many choices before them. The decisions they face can appear overwhelming. Youth need practical ways to connect faith and life, but these practical connections can be difficult to make on their own.

Part of the problem here has to do with the complexity of modern North American society. Youth have always worried about finding a good job, being able to support themselves, and choosing a meaningful direction in life. In contemporary society, however, youth often face a bewildering array of options. Vocational and occupational tracks are constantly changing; many require specialized training or technical knowledge. The sheer complexity of the options makes it more difficult for contemporary youth to see how their faith might help them sort through the decision process. As a result, youth are often confused and unable to focus on a specific vision for their future.

The rift between technical training and spiritual vision has deep cultural roots as well. We live in a society where the separation of church and state has had a long and important history. The principle of separation has worked in many ways to keep religion and political power from interfering with or undermining each other. At the same time, separation has sometimes, and perhaps increasingly, been practiced in ways that effectively relegate religion to the fringes of society. Public schools teach the intellect, the physical, and to a certain degree, the emotional; but they have very few models for even touching on issues related to spirituality. As a result, young people are implicitly trained to separate what they are learning in their various academic studies from what they are learning in faith.

For these and other reasons, youth (and adults as well) often struggle to find ways to connect faith and life. Schools, churches, and other institutions help them to think practically, strategically, and knowledgeably about different "parts of the pie," but youth still need practical ways to integrate all of the pieces, to see life whole, to have a vision and goal for the future. In a word, they need a mentor — someone who will serve as a practical model of what it means to connect faith and life.

A mentoring relationship is a place where a young person can see faith in practice. Since mentoring requires the development of a personal relationship between the adult and the youth, it provides a special opportunity for the youth to see in person what faith looks like in practice. Often persons learn more from observing the *behavior* of others than from their words. This is especially true of spiritual values and moral behavior. Teachers at school provide information about academic subjects. Sunday school teachers often provide information about religious subjects — Christian beliefs, stories, and history. But youth also need to learn by putting beliefs into practice, and by observing the life practice of adults.

Note well, this does not mean that adult mentors must be highly trained observers of culture in order to help youth in this way. Indeed, the most important factor is that the adult is simply willing to be present. When youth are given the opportunity to experience this kind of relationship with an adult, the results can be transforming. Youth are impressed with those who have survived growing up, who have stayed active in the church, and who can be candid about the doubts and struggles of life. The wisdom gained through personal relationship helps youth to see that adults struggle with faith even as youth do. This can help a young person accept his or her own struggle with the integration of faith and life. In this setting, the youth learns to emulate not so much the knowledge or training of the adult, but the pattern and attitude of living. At the same time, when an adult responds to the questions of youth in this way — with candor and wisdom — the youth will only listen to and watch that adult more closely.

Some adults may need convincing that they have anything to offer in this area. After all, the factors that make it difficult for youth to connect faith and life also affect adults. Simply by virtue of being adult, however, and having lived and worked in the world, adults have much to offer. Just imagine, for example, what it can mean to a young person to have an adult listen to one's list of fears and doubts, and then to share a simple response of faith and encouragement. This alone tells the youth that he or she can make it through these problems, that things are not as unmanageable as they seem, that God can be trusted with the future.

At the same time, adults may also have specific expertise to offer. As a result of their involvement in various occupations and professions, adults can model for youth the appropriateness of these occupations for Christians. Youth (especially youth who are serious about their faith) often struggle with whether or not they can serve God effectively in a "secular" field. Youth need models of Christians in the workplace. A recent study commissioned by the Girl Scouts of America showed that relationships with significant adults beyond the environments of home and school play an important role in helping youth understand the moral and institutional fabric of society.[17] Just knowing an adult Christian who is also an artist, or a carpenter, or a computer programmer, or any other occupation, can be a source of great insight and encouragement for youth.

As an example, consider the story of Sally, who was having trouble with school. She did not want to study more than was absolutely necessary. Dates took time from her study and work, and she often could not make up her mind as to which boy to date, preferring to "play the field." She experimented with alcohol and other drugs. Soon she started skipping school and finally dropped out. She drifted from job to job for awhile, never finding one that quite suited her. Then she changed: She decided that she wanted to be a lawyer and to work with the homeless. She went back to school, got good grades, and eventually enrolled in law school.

What changed? Sally found a vision for her life. She found something in herself that had simply been covered over by all the options and activities of growing up. The change came when she began to meet with an adult mentor from the church. The mentor in this case was a businesswoman. More important, the mentor modeled compassion for Sally and eventually encouraged her to go with the church youth group on a mission project to help the homeless. While on that project, doing the mundane work of painting, building, and cleaning up for others, Sally watched her mentor and others in action and caught a vision for her own life. Now she works to make that vision a reality for her future.

Growing into maturity is more than a matter of gaining knowledge, it is also a pilgrimage. Christ came into the world to live a human life, in part to help us with our own pilgrimage. He came to provide a model for life, to be a mentor to his first disciples and to all those who have followed since. Adult mentors follow Christ in this task. As one writer put it, "They, in a sense, assume the awesome role of the ancient novice masters, who traveled to the heights and the depths, who suffered but survived numerous initiation experiences in their own lives, and who, therefore, were chosen to show the path to adulthood."[18]

BENEFITS FOR ADULT MENTORS

We have spoken thus far about some of the benefits of mentoring for youth, for parents, and for the ministry of the church. The benefits of mentoring also extend to those who serve as adult mentors.

While contributing to the self-esteem of youth, for example, adults often find that their own self-esteem is enriched. One of the best ways to select mentoring partners (see pages 31-37) is to allow youth in the congregation to identify prospective adult mentors. Almost without exception, when adults are identified in this way, they experience a sense of honor and pleasure. Many adults have misgivings about the quality of their own Christian experience and witness. How special to have the way you live your life affirmed by a youth! This young person has seen something in you that speaks of what he or she wants to become as a Christian. It is indeed an honor of the highest order to be selected as a role model for faith.

Adults also gain self-confidence from building a relationship with a youth. Adults sometimes lose contact with younger people. Some adults have little opportunity to interact with teens. Either they do not have children of their own, or their children are grown, or the children are not yet teens. As a result, the adults seldom relate with youth, and they may lose confidence in their ability to do so. A relationship with a teenager can, however, be a most enjoyable and enlightening experience. It can remind an adult of interesting dimensions of his or her own life, and build confidence about relating to other people in general.

Likewise, mentoring can have significant results in terms of the faith development of adult mentors. Mentors often learn from their friends in faith. Seeing a faith issue through a new pair of eyes may cause us to look more closely at our belief system. Adults are often stirred by youth who are struggling for consistency in their faith and life. Youth have an ability to get to the heart of issues, to cut through the mire of reasons or excuses we establish for ourselves. They may ask questions that challenge our basic concepts or provide insights we had missed. Many youth are alive with questions, pushing the frontiers of thought and faith. Adults who have been lulled into a world where their faith has not changed much are often called to grow again as they see youth wrestle with the world.

Most of us, unless faced with a crisis, spend little time thinking about our faith. We know what we believe (sort of), we pray and attend worship; but we seldom have occasion to verbalize just what it is that our faith means. Serving as a mentor requires us to focus on the core of our beliefs, and challenges us to put those beliefs into words and actions.

Consider the case of one woman who reluctantly agreed to serve as a mentor. Just prior to the first meeting with her friend in faith, this woman lost her husband. It was a sudden death, and she was experiencing stages of grief. She was angry with God. She called her pastor and said, "This will not work. I'm not in any position to talk to this person about my faith — not now, not when I'm not sure where I am." Her pastor encouraged her to go ahead with the meeting. An interesting thing happened. She could not hide from the youth her feelings of anger, mistrust, and betrayal. This youth took over and became — for that day — her teacher, and talked to her of his faith in God. This woman cried to think that a youth could have that much insight and could see God's presence in all of her grief.

To sit down and really look at our beliefs in the light of a relationship with a youth can help us sort through all the peaks and valleys of our faith. It provides a time to look back on our journey and to revisit experiences that have shaped us into the Christians we are today. On what occasions did we doubt? When did we feel God's presence? What aspects of our faith set us apart as Christians in our decision making? As mentors, we do not have all the answers; nor do we need to claim that we do. Sometimes we may simply acknowledge that we don't know the answer to our own struggle. Viewing faith — with all of its highs and lows, its strengths and weaknesses, its mountains and valleys — from the perspective of a mentoring relationship may give us new insight into who we are as Christians.

How long has it been since you listened to the faith stories of someone older or younger than yourself? Have you ever really listened to how another person feels about God's love? Have you ever discussed with another person his or her fears and doubts? Talking with a young person about his or her faith can give you an entirely new approach to your own.

CONGREGATIONAL LIFE

The benefits we have named are interconnected and cumulative. When youth are helped, adults are helped. When parents are helped, the church is strengthened. When the church improves the quality of its ministry, the surrounding community will also be affected. Indeed, the healing of relationships between the generations is one of the great needs in our society, and mentoring youth in the church can play an important role in this wider healing. To be sure, other benefits might be named and analyzed, but what we finally need to see is the larger picture of healing and wholeness in and through the congregation. Let me try to paint this picture by means of a concluding parable.

There once was a dying monastery. Monks no longer came to spend lives in prayer and service. Try as they might, the remaining monks could not maintain the beautiful old monastery. One of the elder monks sought the sage advice of a rabbi in a nearby town. The rabbi said he had no answer, but he did know that one of the monks in that monastery was the Christ. The old monk returned overjoyed with this incredible news, and all who lived there began to wonder and guess which of them was the Christ. Then a strange thing began to happen. Each monk began to live as though he might be the Christ, and each treated the others as though they might be. Soon things in the monastery started to change. People in the nearby village took notice of the special love and kindness that the monks showed, and word began to spread. Monks once again came to be a part of this now-thriving monastery.[19]

A mentoring ministry in your congregation will not solve every problem or guarantee a miraculous turnaround. It will, however, offer your members — youth and adults — the opportunity to discover anew what it means to be the Body of Christ to one another. As persons participate in the mentoring program, they become visible symbols for the entire congregation of Christ's presence and power. As church members see youth and adults grow and learn together, they also gain a vision for the continuity of faith through the ages. In this way, mentoring provides a sense of unity in the congregation, and a witness to the wider world that the spirit of Christ is alive and active in our midst.

When we begin to think and act in Christlike ways toward one another, it shows. Word spreads about the special love and kindness we exhibit and live out. People begin to notice and to talk about the love and kindness shown at this particular church. A church can be like the monastery. A church in which youth and adults are prepared to care for and love one another is in a position to care for and love the world as well. That church can be a mentoring church.

3 | STEPS

IF YOU WANT TO EXPLORE the benefits of mentoring in your congregation, you will need to consider taking some specific steps. How will you go about raising the interest of the congregation in the mentoring ministry? In what settings will you incorporate mentoring into the life of the church? What role will be played in all of this by your pastor and a mentoring team? Your response to these and other questions will determine in large measure the effectiveness of your mentoring ministry.

CREATE A DESIGN TEAM

When starting a mentoring program in your congregation, the first step is to put together a planning team. This team is typically composed of the pastor and a committee of leaders who agree to give direction to the ministry. Naturally, you will want to clear the vision for the ministry with the council on ministries, education committee, board of discipleship, and whomever else should be advised about special programs. The importance of church-wide excitement about the mentoring program cannot be overstated.

As with most events in a local church, the pastor's support is crucial. The primary role of the pastor, however, is not to be a mentor, but to support those who are. The pastor initiates the program. He or she meets with the design team and approves the resources and plans that will be used. Indeed, experience has shown that congregational support for the ministry will depend in large measure on the pastor's involvement with the design team, especially during the initial stages of planning and preparation.

With the support of the pastor and other administrative bodies of the congregation, the design team will establish the program and monitor progress. The team should include the pastor, the youth coordinator, two parents, and two youth workers or teachers. It may be smaller if few youth will be involved in the program. The team should meet and have the entire program planned before the program actually starts. This ministry takes considerable start-up energy, and it is important that the program start strong. Once the program is going, it runs itself quite well. The pastor's energy is needed less as the program develops. By the second year, the pastor's involvement may decrease significantly as more persons become trained and are able to carry a larger part of the responsibility. (A model for a basic Planner's Workshop is included in Appendix A, page 74. Adapt this model as needed in order to present the idea of mentoring to an initial group of interested persons and to invite them to enter into the planning process with you.)

RELATE THE MENTORING PROGRAM TO OTHER MINISTRIES

One of the first steps your design team will want to consider in some detail is the relation of your mentoring ministry to other ongoing ministries of your congregation. In Chapters 1 and 2 we mentioned that mentoring can and should be related to other aspects of the Christian education program, such as confirmation, Sunday school, and regular youth meetings. Let's look now at some of these options in more detail.

The most common use of the mentoring program in United Methodist congregations is with a confirmation class. The practice of confirmation has a variety of theological roots and may differ significantly between denominations. Most churches combine several basic ideas in their views of confirmation. Some of these basic ideas include: the beginning of life-long discipleship, personally affirming vows made for us at our baptism, membership training, initiating youth into adulthood in the church, awareness of a conversion experience, and a preparatory time prior to the decision to join the church. No matter how it is presented, however, confirmation is important in the life of the church, and mentoring can be transformative in the process of confirmation.

In relation to confirmation (or profession of faith class), mentoring focuses in particular on younger adolescents. As part of this experience, the church places a caring and spiritually mature adult with each youth. The purpose is that they will explore faith together. In the past, confirmation classes have often been too formal and too short to provide the indepth discussion available through a mentoring program. The mentoring experience, by contrast, can enhance the confirmation class by providing a time for each youth to speak privately with an adult friend about faith questions raised in class. It also provides an opportunity to discuss other questions not raised in class at all. Mentoring partners can test the class learnings in the real world. The mentor can tell about his or her own life experiences that relate to confirmation issues.

As we mentioned in Chapter 2, a mentoring program in the context of confirmation can do much to bring the church alive. A church that participates in a mentoring ministry involves several persons (parents, mentors, pastors) in the training process that guides each youth toward a meaningful decision about faith and church membership. This participation spreads throughout the congregation, giving more persons ownership and pride in the spiritual growth of young lives. Mentoring helps persons feel they are part of the ministry of nurturing and spiritual formation. More persons — both youth and adults — become aware of how faith is passed from one generation to another. Confirmation is no longer something that happens to youth while the rest of the congregation watches. Confirmation now becomes a special church event in which candidates — whom "we" helped to guide — make a decision. Youth discover in a personal way the value of the faith that their church teaches. Participating in a worship service where a confirmation class joins the membership of the church can be a joyful experience; knowing that the adult members of your congregation (perhaps including yourself) have been personally engaged in the process of molding and shaping the faith of these youth brings joy of an even greater order.

Current confirmation programs in several denominations have begun to include mentoring. As a result, the practice of confirmation in these congregations is being transformed. Youth and adults have begun to recognize more deeply and powerfully that confirmation is the beginning of lifelong discipleship, not simply a momentary rite of passage. Confirmation is not an ending, but rather a new step in a lifelong journey. Baptism marks the beginning of an affiliation with the church as a member of the Body of Christ. Confirmation offers the youth an opportunity to personally claim that membership. The story of Jack and Henry in Chapter 1 is from one such confirmation class.

From the standpoint of the local church, this means that a mentoring ministry will help you and your congregation live out your vows through the mentors. Each baptized person can have a mentor. The mentor's responsibility is to help the parents raise the child or youth into Christian maturity. Do not expect that anyone presenting her or himself for baptism is a mature Christian. It may be that each of us needs a mentor all of our lives. We need to grow and expand in our faith, and mentors help us do that.

In addition to confirmation, mentoring can also work effectively in a variety of other settings. In the setting of a particular Sunday school class, for example, mentoring might be part of the curriculum or a supplement to it. Church school classes can use mentoring to increase the youth's interest in the curriculum. Class discussion often improves as a result. Consider the case of Julie and Wilma.

Julie and Wilma became involved in a mentoring experience as a part of a Sunday school program. Julie was in the junior high class, and Wilma was in an adult class. Each class adopted the other for a period of time. Both classes studied the same general curriculum. Julie and Wilma were surprised to find that they were dealing with the same basic life issues. Both were concerned about their relationship to God, their personal integrity, what the church meant to them, and their values and beliefs. They had much to discuss and contemplate. They talked, prayed, and played together. Each grew in her personal and community faith.

Another option is more comprehensive. Some churches provide for each of their youth a mentoring experience unconnected to any other particular program. At a specific age, each youth becomes involved in a mentoring experience. Churches that have developed a mentoring program for all of their youth generally believe that the program is necessary to the nurturing process for each youth, no matter what her or his participation in other parts of church life might be.

Other mentoring possibilities include adults with other adults. They might be experienced teachers with new teachers, established mentors with new members, or new leaders with persons presently holding positions. Mentoring relationships have also been successful between children and youth and sometimes between youth and other youth. (Some of these options are explored in more detail in Appendix B: Mentoring Possibilities, page 77.)

PRESENT THE PLAN TO THE CONGREGATION

Once you have located the mentoring ministry in relation to other existing ministries and received approval for your basic plan from the administrative bodies of your congregation, your next step is to present the developing concept to the congregation as a whole. A mentoring ministry works best when the whole congregation is aware of and supports what is happening.

The pastor and the design team should make a presentation to the whole church. This presentation might be part of a church family supper, a special called meeting, or some other appropriate session. The pastor and team should assign various tasks that will be involved in the presentation. Who will be in charge of planning the meeting? When and where will the meeting be held? How will people be invited to attend the meeting, and what opportunities to respond will be given?

Along with basic meeting plans, you will also want to give special attention to the central motivational part of your presentation. Experience has shown that people respond most favorably when the ideas for new ministries are presented in one of several ways. Naturally you will want to use various of your usual media — bulletin boards, newsletters, and others. These are important for keeping the members of the church informed. These are places to which all members will turn at one time or another. They will need to be augmented, however, in order to really build a vision for the ministry in your congregation.

One way to introduce mentoring to your congregation is to invite key leaders to visit another church where a mentoring program is already in progress. At a leisure ministry workshop several years ago, Walter Kimbrough, an Atlanta pastor, revealed how he got persons excited about a new idea. He finds a church where the program is in operation. He then invites key persons from his own church to visit the program with him. The end result is that many persons in the church are excited about the program.

Sometimes visiting a place where something important is happening is the only way to understand a vision. We often spend many hours trying to convince youth that some program will be exciting, meaningful, and worthwhile, almost expecting a "ho-hum" response. Workcamps are a good example. When trying to start workcamps, the general response is, "Why would I want to give a week of my time sleeping on the floor in an unairconditioned gym with cold showers, to work all day in the hot sun tarpapering a roof? You've got to be kidding." After they return from doing just that, the youth are full of enthusiasm for the project and for their interaction with the persons involved. They just did not understand the vision before.

"You just had to be there," is a common phrase. "You just had to see it for yourself. I can't explain it." One of the best ways to introduce any new program to the church is to take a group of key persons to a place where the program is working. Let the persons see the program in operation, ask questions of those involved, and see others witness to the things that can be done. The visitors then return with a vision that they can relate to the congregation as a whole. They will provide enormous energy and will want to move along rapidly.

Yet another way to introduce mentoring to your congregation is to bring a mentor to your church. The first time I wanted to involve my local church in a mentoring program, I invited a group from another church that had offered a mentoring program for several years. A mentor, a youth, and the pastor came and told their stories. The youth spoke of the importance of having someone in whom to confide. The mentor said she entered the relationship with misgivings, but the new relationship made her examine her life and faith in new ways. The pastor told how the program had a tremendous effect on the whole congregation. Each of these witnesses showed in very personal ways how the mentoring ministry had deepened the faith and involvement of many people in this congregation.

INVITE YOUTH TO PARTICIPATE

With a growing sense of structure and publicity, you are ready to move forward with the process of inviting specific youth to participate in the program. Inviting persons to be in the mentoring program takes time and caring. The inviting process is twofold: inviting youth and inviting mentors. Much of the inviting process is the same for both groups. We shall discuss the process of inviting and training adults to become mentors in more detail below. Naturally, some of these steps will overlap in time with the process of inviting youth. For now, let's focus on the process of inviting youth.

To begin with, your design team will need to discover the names of *all* youth related to the congregation who are in the target age group. If you plan to use mentoring only in the confirmation process, this will create one list of names. If you plan a more comprehensive program, then your list will expand accordingly. In any event, the pastor should work with the design team to determine which youth to invite into the mentoring program each year. In order to reach all potential candidates with at least one consistent message, it will be a good idea for the pastor and the design team to compose a form letter that goes out to the entire list.

The easiest part of this task is to identify all youth who are currently active in the church. Records for church school, youth choir, pre-membership rolls, etc., will supply most of these names. Somewhat more difficult is the task of identifying inactive and prospective youth. Records for Scouts, sports activities, vacation church school, and other documents, as well as memory and word of mouth, may be required to identify these other potential candidates for the mentoring program. In any case, it is important to identify all potential candidates so that no one feels ignored or left out.

The role of the pastor can be crucial in the invitation process, especially at the beginning of a new program. The pastor is someone most youth regard as a leader in the congregation. Likewise, adults (parents and mentors) look to the pastor for guidance and empowerment. The pastor models caregiving, teaching, and faith formation. The pastor's involvement places high value on the program and gives it a strong start.

We use the word *invite* on purpose. A word the church has used for many years is *recruit*. Recruiting persons often carries negative images. When I think of recruiting, I think of the military or of someone trying to get me to do something I really do not want to do. People usually recruit by leaving out important things or saying the job is easier than it really is. My inclination when someone wants to recruit me is to say no.

The word *invite* is much more positive. It resonates with thoughts of parties, friendly conversations, and special events. We think of doing something fun and important, of responding to a need that can use our talents. We generally respond favorably to invitations. Often we can create in ourselves a positive or negative image based on the label we put on what we are doing.

While doing research for his book, *Inviting Youth*, Bill Wolfe interviewed youth all over the United States about how they like to be invited to something. The overwhelming preference was that the invitation be extended "personally."[20] We often prefer the easiest, least time-consuming way to invite persons, the favorite method being the form letter. Yet if we take seriously the interviewed youth, that is not enough. Youth, like adults, tend to evaluate the importance of an event by how they are invited. When persons take time to come to my house and invite me personally, I know they are really interested in me.

For this reason it will not be enough for the pastor and the design team to simply send a form letter of invitation to all possible youth. Youth should receive a personal invitation in addition to the letters. If we want youth to say "yes," then we must give them reason to say it. This may be one of the most important decisions in their lives.

A committee member and a youth who has previously been through the mentoring program make the best in-person inviting team. For churches just starting this process, the inviting team might include members of the design team and prospective mentors, since, by this point, they will have received a good deal of information. When Jesus invited his disciples to follow, he did not send form letters. He invited them in person. He engaged them where they were and called them. Mentors and friends in faith need this same personal, caring touch.

Bill Wolfe also discovered in his interviews that people respond best to invitations when they feel that they have a unique contribution to make, or that they will receive benefits uniquely tuned to who they are.[21] Drawing on the benefits mentioned in Chapter 2, your inviting team can appeal to youth in several ways. Each youth is invited into a unique opportunity, a ministry tailored to each person's situation. The youth's special interests and questions will be an integral part of the experience. The youth will have personal "one-on-one" time with an individual he or she trusts and respects. The youth will affect the mentor and the mentor's faith. Indeed, the youth will have an important role to play in selecting the specific individual who will serve as his or her mentor.

INVITE ADULTS TO BE MENTORS

The process of inviting adults to become mentors is one of the most important steps you will take in the formation of your mentoring ministry. Mentors must be persons who appeal to youth, but also to parents and other adults. In the next chapter we shall look at a number of skills mentors need in order to be effective. Keep these skills in mind as you consider specific people for this important role. Just here, however, let's look at some specific steps in the selection process.

The first step in the selection process is to allow youth to have a voice in the process of identifying potential mentoring partners. Ask the youth of your congregation to think about the adults in the congregation, and to submit names of adults whose lives and character they admire. Since a specific youth's first choice may not be able to serve, ask each youth to identify several adults as potential mentors. You might incorporate this step into your participant's workshop (see page 37 and Appendix C, page 82). The results can be surprising. In one church, for example, the mentoring program was to include seven youth. All seven named the same person as one of their choices. He was an eighty-year-old man who, as far as could be determined, had never been formally involved with youth. What unique spark attracted youth to this man's faith? For several weeks I observed him. I discovered that he was an avid reader of the local newspaper, reading from first page to last. At church on Sunday he engaged in conversation with every person whose name or family name appeared in the newspaper the previous week — adult, youth, or child. With youth or children whose names did not appear, he asked about things at school. This man remembered specifics. Anyone who encountered this octogenarian would think he had been present at whatever event had taken place. I suspect that over a month's time he spoke with every member of the church, and talked to every youth at least a couple of times.

The woman at the well must have been amazed at Jesus, because he seemed to know all about her. The youth of this church must have been equally impressed by this man who conversed with them about things they would not expect him to know. He did it in a way that made them feel he was interested rather than nosy. Youth who often felt unimportant or unwanted in the church were attracted to this man. I understood why they chose him. But when invited to be a mentor, he was completely surprised. His response was, "I don't know how to work with youth. I've never taught or gone on outings. I never had any children. I don't think I would know what to do." I reminded him of his ways of conversing with everyone, including youth. He was flattered and surprised that what he did was so important. He felt good that the youth liked him. Later, he made a super mentor.

One reason few adults decline the invitation to serve is the sense of honor and pleasure they feel at having been nominated by youth. Like the octogenarian described above, most adults are flattered and surprised that youth would choose them to serve as mentors. Some adults may not have worked with youth before and may not realize they have a special relationship with youth. When presented with a personal invitation, however, they will realize that youth have seen something special in them. Many will be willing to serve. The main problem may be to decide which youth gets to have which adult as his or her first choice.

On the basis of the names the youth identify, the pastor and design team can move forward with the selection of actual mentors. Mentors need to be persons who care for others and who know how to accept significant responsibility. Therefore, your inviting team should also be composed of caring persons. Caring persons will help potential mentors understand the full range of responsibilities and benefits — short-term and long-range — that serving offers to all of those who get involved.

For one thing, your inviting team will want to help the potential mentor see the value of serving. Mentors need to know that they themselves will grow from the process. To this end, the inviter might tell stories about other mentors, about how they have grown and benefited. You can use some of the stories included in this volume or, if possible, include veteran mentors from previous classes as part of your inviting team. Hearing the story of an experienced mentor is one of the most powerful ways to convey the vision. Ask that the stories be told in a low-key, informal manner. Few prospects say no to the opportunity; in fact, most are excited about this kind of involvement with youth.

Likewise, the caring inviter listens to the potential mentor. When I was first appointed to a church as an associate pastor, I was responsible for inviting a large number of church school teachers. The senior pastor and I were together on one particular call. About halfway through the visit, I realized the potential teacher had tried to speak several times. We were so intent on making our "pitch" before she had a chance to say "no," we just kept talking. Since then I have learned the importance of caring through listening and being open to the concerns of others.

In addition, mentors need to understand the job responsibilities and potential workload that will be required. What are the specific time expectations? How often should they plan to meet with the friend in faith? How long is a typical meeting? What other activities might they consider as ways of improving and strengthening the relationship? The purpose is not to overwhelm, but to outline both the opportunities and the responsibilities. (See also the discussion of schedules for mentoring in Chapter 5, page 52.)

A mentor must be able to make regular contact and keep appointments with the friend in faith, or the youth will conclude that the mentor does not care. One mentor never quite made contact. A member of the choir, every Sunday after worship he went first to the choir room to change his robe, then back to the sanctuary to find his friend in faith. The youth, however, had to leave with his family every Sunday immediately after worship in order to take lunch to his homebound grandmother. The mentor really did care, but he did not fully understand the responsibilities involved. He thought this was something he could do for a few minutes on Sunday at church. Unaware that the mentor had even been trying to meet with him, the youth lost interest and concluded that the mentor just did not care.

One of the most basic criteria for the selection process of a mentor is a sense of calling. We are called by God to do many things in this world — probably many more than we are aware of. Being called is not always easily discerned. It is, however, important to link our actions with a sense of God's will for our lives. When we do things for and with God's creation, we do them for and with God. We don't always get specific messages about which part of God's creation to be involved with, but the general message is clear. God has given us talents and abilities as part of God's call for us.

When a youth says that he or she admires my faith and would like to pattern his or her life after mine, I have a responsibility to that youth; but also a greater responsibility to God's will for me in the world. God has called me to care for others. Here is someone asking for my care. I must respond to the person and to what God asks of me. Is this the one, Lord?

God's call is not always direct, often calling through another individual or event. In the inviting process it is important to ask a person to think about whether this is part of God's call for her or him as an individual. The inviter does not have that information. Only the invited person can find the answer. Arm twisting will not help. Let God do the convincing. Our responsibility is to help the prospect see the possibilities.

As part of the invitation process in United Methodist congregations, it can also be helpful to invite adults to reflect on the vows the congregation takes when persons are baptized.[22] This is not intended to obligate them to be mentors. Rather it is a call to discipleship, a call for them to be aware of what they have pledged, and an opportunity to consider mentoring as a way to fulfill that pledge. When any person is baptized, other members of the congregation pledge to nurture that person in faith — whether infant, youth, or adult. In far too many congregations, this becomes an idle pledge. Being part of a mentoring ministry is one way to take such pledges seriously and faithfully.

Some congregations go a step further by linking the ministry of mentoring with the actual rite of baptism. Mentors are identified before baptism takes place. The mentor stands with the baptized person's family and takes the congregational vows with them. The mentoring role and the vow to nurture new Christians from the time of their baptism are thus tied together. The mentor does not act *instead* of the congregation, just with more intensity. The vow of the entire congregation is still valid as all members are called to aid in the nurture of this person.

At the same time, it is important that the pastor and the design team exercise wisdom in the process of selecting and confirming the call of potential mentors. Above all, leaders must understand that no one can train persons in a short time to love others, to get along with youth, to have a mature faith, and to be morally and ethically sound. To be sure, instruction and training can help — that is why we discuss training on pages 38-41 — but good mentoring skills run deeper than training alone can accomplish. They are the product of lifelong habits. That is why we devote the entire next chapter to this subject.

In this light, inviting adults to become mentors requires making some judgment calls. Asking youth to participate in the selection process helps a lot. Just being chosen by a youth suggests that a person has some skills in getting along with youth. On the other hand, youth sometimes choose persons who for one reason or another lack the integrity and capabilities to be good mentors. Youth selections need to be confirmed. Acceptance into the program does not insure the potential mentor's goodness or relationship with God. Nor does a decision not to include someone mean that he or she is unfit. Choosing mentors requires determining who are the *best* persons for the mentoring program.

One pastor had to make a tough decision. A person nominated by a youth as a mentor had been accused on two different occasions of sexual advances to persons in the church. He had neither been accused publicly nor charged with the offense. When the pastor talked with the man, he denied the accusations. No public judgment should or could be made in Christian love, yet the situation was too uncertain to match this man in a one-on-one situation with a youth. So the pastor had to decide against using this man as a mentor, because the unanswered question was too serious.

Persons should be invited out of love and genuine care, not mechanically. Invite persons because you love them and care enough to express that love. Design your invitation in your own style, allowing God's love to flow through you.

SET SOME SPECIFIC DATES

As awareness of the mentoring program grows in your congregation, you will need to determine some specific dates for key events that lead to the full-scale launch of the ministry. The announcement of these dates can build a sense of momentum even before you have been able to make final determinations concerning which youth and adults will be able to participate in the program.

One date that needs special attention is the initial meeting with interested youth, their parents, some potential mentor candidates, and the pastor(s). This meeting should take place approximately six weeks to two months before the program begins. The design team needs to plan this meeting carefully and announce to the youth, parents, and mentor candidates the time, date, place, and the meeting agenda. (A model for the agenda of this meeting is given in Appendix B: Participant's Workshop, page 77. Adapt this model as needed for your own purposes.)

If your congregation has had previous mentoring classes, then invite former youth participants, mentors, and parents to be part of this new orientation. They, better than anyone else, can explain the purpose and potential of the mentoring program.

In addition, some congregations have planned one or more special worship services to recognize and acknowledge the start-up of a new mentoring class. Plan such a service to focus on the mentoring theme (e.g., the mentoring relationship of Paul and Timothy, or one of the other biblical models of mentoring mentioned in Chapter 1), and announce it well in advance.

Likewise, some churches plan a covenant-making process as part of this service — a time for all members of the congregation to reflect together on the importance of the mentoring ministry, and to commit themselves to helping in every way they can. During the worship service, give people an opportunity to fill out a covenant card and to place it in the offering plate or at the altar. This establishes a covenant among the person signing, God, and the youth of the church. In essence, signing the card indicates that the signer recognizes that youth of the congregation are entering into a new mentoring relationship. Further, the signer is asked to pray for this ministry, to seek opportunities to be open to the youth, and to renew his/her commitment to grow personally in relationships with God and with other persons. In this way the covenant cards show that mentoring is a *congregational* ministry.

TRAIN AND SUPPORT MENTORS

As potential mentors emerge from your selection process, you and your design team will need to move forward with the process of confirming and training them. Part of this will simply be to strengthen the gifts you and the youth have already recognized in these persons. You might, for example, encourage mentors to read and reflect on the list of skills given in the next chapter. In addition to these skills, however, your mentors may also need information and training in some specific areas. Naturally this training will occur well before the first meetings between mentors and youth.

Each person who accepts the invitation to be a mentor needs an orientation or short training period. For one thing, mentors need to know something about the basic stages of faith development. People sometimes mistakenly assume that others have had the same growth experiences they have had, or that new Christians are at the same level of Christian maturity as all other Christians. Information on the ways faith develops and the level of faith that might be expected from persons at various age levels can be extremely helpful to the mentors.

Mentoring is one way for the church to enable a young person to profess faith in God and in Jesus Christ. It is important, however, for the mentor to realize that there is more than this one way for a youth to come to faith. The way the mentor came to faith may or may not be repeated in the experience of the youth. Some people are deeply impressed by an intellectual presentation of the gospel. Others may need an experience of emotional healing before faith can take root in significant ways. Yet others must first take some step of moral change before they can even see the point of Christian beliefs. As the friends in faith begin to share their stories of faith, they will see these and other general patterns emerge; yet mentors need to know that each person's story will be also be unique in some ways.

Theories concerning the stages of faith can be controversial. Jim Fowler and John Westerhoff have both offered theories to help us understand what happens as people grow in faith.[23] Mentors do not have to accept any particular theory in order to be effective in ministry; but they do need to be clear that their experiences are not necessarily those that youth have to have.

As persons of mature faith, mentors may be prone to be somewhat comfortable in their faith position. Perhaps the mentor has reached a plateau in faith. The mentored person, by contrast, is apt to be in a transition or searching period of faith growth. This does not necessarily lead to conflict, but it does require understanding. The youth may ask questions or challenge elements of faith that the mentor settled long ago. The tone and manner of the mentor's response at such a time can make a crucial impression on the young person. Mentors need to understand that all questions are acceptable insofar as they represent real concerns of the questioner. An answer that is satisfactory to the mentor, moreover, may not speak to the youth. The role of the mentor in such cases is to help the seeker discover an answer that makes sense to his or her own understanding. Enabling faith growth means understanding that persons are different and that answers always involve personal perspectives. The goal is to help another to grasp his or her own faith in God through Christ, not to force that person into the mentor's faith.

To help mentors understand that youth are diverse in many ways, training should address issues of cultural heritage and family background as these reflect on the nature of individual mentoring relationships.

In one case study, for example, a mentor needed to understand the family background of the friend in faith in order to appreciate the youth's struggle with trusting God. The mentor and the youth had been discussing their relationships with God. The mentor noticed that the youth seemed to picture God as a terrible, forceful, vengeful being who did not really care or love. As the discussion progressed, the mentor discovered that this youth's image of God was connected in her mind with family memories, and with the fact that the church often uses the word *Father* to address God. This young woman had had three different father figures in her fifteen years. Her biological father, whom she loved dearly as a young girl, left one day without saying good-bye and never returned. Her second father beat her, and the courts removed him from the family. Her third father was often absent, traveling most of the time as part of his job. As a result, this youth had never really developed a positive image of God as "Father." Her case is extreme, but it illustrates how personal and cultural experiences can affect the faith development of youth.

For this reason, mentor training should make an effort to distinguish between faith and culture. All Christians hold their faith to some extent within the boundaries of a particular culture and a history of personal experience. Our understandings of faith are always influenced by factors such as age, race, family, class, geography, and gender; but none of these factors can be identified simplistically with faith. Mentors need to understand that faith can find expression in many different kinds of cultures; yet it resists every culture at some points. Therefore, the goal of mentoring is to help persons grow in faith within their own cultures, not to require allegiance to our own.

Likewise, mentors need to understand something of the physical and emotional development of youth at different age levels. Physical changes are one of the most powerful forces in the lives of youth. They grow in spurts — sometimes appearing to be all arms and legs. They begin to manifest adult sexual characteristics. Their voices change and they are often self-conscious. Girls mature faster than boys, and may see boys as immature. They form intense friendships, especially with the same sex. They are trying to discover who they are in the transition between childhood and adulthood. This search often includes confusion and mood swings. They tend to be insecure and long for acceptance. They can, however, develop relationships with older persons. They are willing to converse about themselves and their ideas in a safe environment. Religious experiences are important to them. They are a mixed bag of physical and emotional upheaval. Any information that can help adult mentors understand these kinds of changes will be most welcome.

This is perhaps a natural place to address another important though sensitive aspect of mentor training: issues related to child abuse. Because mentoring involves a personal relationship between an adult and a youth, the mentor must pay attention to matters of courtesy, decency, and appearance. The way the relationship *looks* can be just as important as the way it *is*. Meetings with youth should occur in public places, such as parks, restaurants, shopping malls, and other places where persons can talk privately yet be seen publicly. When meeting in the home of either mentor or youth, another family member should be present (even if in another room).

There are several reasons for this caution. Persons unaware of the mentor relationship might imagine sexual involvement and mention the idea to others, creating a fictitious and potentially damaging scenario. Parents may feel more comfortable if their child is not alone with an adult mentor, at least until they get to know each other better. All concerned need to be reassured that the relationship is one of faith and friendship, and that it is open to observation.

It is also important to minimize the possibility of actual abuse taking place within the mentor relationship. Choosing reliable people to serve as mentors is reassuring, but that is simply a first step. Youth are usually taught what abuse is and how to avoid and report it. Mentors also need to be given a few tips. If the mentor hugs too soon, the gesture might be misinterpreted and the relationship either ended or hindered. Teach mentors how to hug and touch in appropriate ways and urge them to do this only in public. Try not to overemphasize this caution or scare people. Just make the mentors aware of their responsibility to set a good example and to practice some caution.

As your mentoring program develops, you will want to provide continued training and support for your mentors. The pastor in particular can play an important role in supporting mentors by being available to help with questions or problems. In this way the pastor can serve as mentor to the mentors. Mentors should be encouraged to call on the pastor in order to discuss their own faith and commitment. They need to know that they are doing the right thing. Don't let mentors become isolated from the pastor, the design team, or from each other. You might even plan periodic luncheons or dinners to bring the mentors together to share what they are learning.

SUPPORT PARENTS AND KEEP THEM INFORMED

In any program where youth and adults are involved, it is important for adult leaders to keep parents informed and up to date. Once again the pastor has a key role to play, keeping the parents informed of the youth's progress in the program and answering questions as they arise. Parents are often curious about their youth's involvement with a mentor. Often their offspring do not tell them much. Since the mentor's role includes keeping confidences (at least up to a certain point), he or she cannot be the parents' main source of information.

The pastor can assure parents that if conversations between the youth and the mentor indicate anything of potential danger to the youth or to the family, the mentor will encourage the youth to talk about it with the pastor. If the youth is unwilling and abuse is suspected, the mentor should go with the pastor to the appropriate authority as prescribed by law. This is rare, and in most congregations this will not happen. If it does, the pastor enables the proper help. The pastor needs to be available for these serious issues. (See also the discussion of confidentiality on pages 51, 67-68, and 70.)

EVALUATE THE MINISTRY

The pastor also helps the design team in the process of evaluation when a particular series of mentoring relationships is complete. The pastor should ensure that the evaluation takes place. Often church members do not evaluate a program, but just continue to do it because they believe that they ought to—or they discontinue the program because it is too much work. Since the pastor starts the process, he or she should be in on all evaluations and recommendations concerning changes or improvements for future programs. The pastor at this juncture serves as a team member rather than as the leader. Thus, in addition to helping launch the program, the pastor has a key role in monitoring the program as it grows and develops.

4 | SKILLS

NOT EVERYONE CAN BE A MENTOR. Mentors should be persons of mature faith who are willing to give of themselves to make mentoring a successful venture. In its study of effective Christian education in six denominations, the Search Institute concluded that a person of mature faith is one who: trusts and believes, experiences the fruits of faith, integrates faith and life, seeks spiritual growth, experiences and nurtures faith in community, holds life-affirming values, advocates social change, acts and serves.[24] In this light, a good mentor will have certain character traits and qualities, such as:

- Visible belief in God
- Willingness to discuss his or her faith
- Genuine caring for persons
- Positive attitude
- Willingness to communicate
- Willingness to support and affirm others
- Willingness to give time to a relationship
- Commitment to moral and ethical standards
- Respect for others' abilities
- Respect for confidentiality
- Compassion for others
- Openness to expect and accept evidence of the presence of the Holy Spirit

In addition to simply naming these traits, however, let's try to grasp several of them in a more substantial way through images, stories, and further definitions.

THE MENTOR AS A HOST

One way to look at the mentor's role is through the image of "host." A good host prizes the freedom of his or her guests, yet accepts a certain responsibility for the guests' well-being. The mentor also must be aware of the freedom of the person mentored to be who he or she is and must take responsibility for initiating much that happens in the time the two are together.

The mentor as host invites and takes the initiative. As host, the mentor does not expect the youth to invite him or herself into a relationship. Throughout the time together the mentor is primarily responsible for the contacts. This does not mean that the youth cannot show initiative; many do, and it is perfectly acceptable. Keeping the image of mentor as host in mind, let's look at some virtues and skills mentors need in order to be effective.

CONFIDENCE

Like any good host, *the mentor needs to be confident.* The fact that the mentor is confident does not necessarily mean that the mentor is comfortable. Many professional stage performers are confident that they know what to do, but are uncomfortable just before the performance. Likewise, many mentors who know what they will do in their next sessions with their youth friends are, nevertheless, anxious and uncomfortable. However, the more at ease the host is, the more the guests can discuss important things.

Our firm and loving God encourages us to grow in faith. Mentors are confident in their faith, because they know that through God's grace they have the opportunity to explore their relationship to God and God's will for them in this life. The knowledge that God loves us as we grow in faith provides confidence in faith. This confidence is part of what the mentor embodies.

Mentors are self-confident. This means that mentors live lives without serious reservations. We are all concerned about things we do. Even Paul was concerned about his "thorn in the flesh." Generally, however, mentors live life with confidence that they are making good decisions.

Mentors like being with others. Few persons are comfortable with everyone they meet, but mentors get along with most people. The mentor likes people, works well with people, spends time with people, and knows that people offer opportunities to learn more about self, God, and the world.

Mentors are confident that God is with them no matter what happens. Mentors know that, in both good times and bad, God is available to help us live with joy. Some things in life bring almost too much joy or sadness for us to bear. The mentor is open to God's help in times of overwhelming good fortune, as well as when life is so terrible it hardly seems worth living.

LEADERSHIP

Likewise, *mentors are leaders*, and they need to practice leadership in relationship with their friends in faith. Before guests arrive, the host selects activities for the time together or plans some options from which the guests may choose. The host is open to new ideas if they arise, but also to the prohibition of activities inappropriate or unwanted in his or her home. Like the host, the mentor is in charge of the schedule when the mentor and youth are together.

The mentor is open to any concerns the youth brings. The mentor encourages the youth to offer conversation topics. However, the mentor must be prepared both to provide topics for discussion when the youth is unable to offer any, and to change the subject when it is inappropriate or an undue diversion.

Often the most difficult time for the mentor is the first meeting. "How do I get started?" is one of the most frequently asked questions in orientation sessions. The easiest introductory session is a visit to the local pizza parlor or other eating establishment. Talking while enjoying a meal seems to work well as a starting point.

A list of ice-breaking questions will help overcome that first hurdle. Keep questions neutral and nonthreatening. Deal with common interests or each other's everyday activities, but progress slowly into areas involving the church and faith. Some sample questions:

- What is your favorite food?
- What is your favorite time of day?
- How do you like to spend Sunday afternoons?
- What was Christmas like when you were ten years old?
- What is your favorite place in the church?

Mentors may add to this list or make up their own questions. In any case, mentors must be sure that questions are nonthreatening, address common interests, and follow a logical progression.

Consider another true account. The first meeting did not go as well as Elizabeth had hoped. Sandra was quite silent, giving only brief answers to questions Elizabeth asked. Being Sandra's mentor had seemed like a good idea. Bringing a youth and an adult together each week over a three-month period to discuss faith together could produce a stronger faith in each person, so Elizabeth was honored and excited to be asked.

Looking back at that first meeting brought smiles and a certain thoughtfulness to Elizabeth. She remembered how nervous she was. As the mentor she was asked to arrange the first meeting. She chose the location after much thought. It needed to provide a relaxing atmosphere where two people who knew each other on sight, had conversed only briefly, and were generally strangers could begin a mutual quest to deepen their faith. The pizza parlor seemed like the most neutral, comfortable place to begin. To be more comfortable, she asked Roy, her husband, to go there with her to try it out a couple of nights beforehand. She agonized over what to wear. She did not want to appear too formal, but also did not want to be so casual that Sandra would think she was condescending to her. Should she pick Sandra up or meet her at the pizza parlor? There were so many questions, and they had not even met yet!

Sandra was a young person full of energy. She was always chatty with her friends and steadily involved in church activities. But when Sandra entered the pizza parlor she seemed different, almost shy. Elizabeth thought Sandra must have had some of the same questions about clothes. She was dressed differently than Elizabeth remembered ever seeing her. Perhaps they had some things in common after all. During the meal there were long silences. Sandra was polite and answered questions, but was slow to offer any conversation. Then Elizabeth confessed her frustration over choosing clothes for this initial meeting. Sandra smiled and the conversation started slowly.

That was many sessions ago. It was hard to remember Sandra's initial shyness. She was now so full of conversation and questions that her energy was contagious. Elizabeth noticed a new measure of energy in herself during and after their meetings. The relationship developed to the point that they talked about faith and almost everything else. Sandra asked tough questions that caused Elizabeth to grow and to know more about herself and the way she responds to life. And Elizabeth talked and asked questions that caused Sandra to think and to change. The mentoring process worked on them both. Sandra sometimes stopped by or called Elizabeth on the phone, but usually Elizabeth arranged their meetings. Elizabeth was the host, and the host plans the party.

The most important leadership the mentor provides is leadership that facilitates sharing personal faith stories. The mentor should be prepared to talk about his or her personal faith journey with all its ups and downs. (See Appendices D and E, pages 86-90.) Everything the friends in faith do together should lead finally to this sharing of personal faith. This sharing does not, however, have to happen immediately. Nor does it come neatly wrapped and ready to publish in a book. Rather the mentor reveals, as appropriate times create the opportunity, his or her own relationship to God and acceptance of Christ. This kind of sharing should unfold as the relationship develops. The mentor's story is about his or her own experiences of God working in life and in the world; it is not an account of the proper way to live. Indeed, the mentor may not believe she or he has done everything in the best way — and that is fine, because each person must find his or her own way in faith.

The mentor's gradual personal revelations invite the friend in faith to tell portions of her or his own story. First discuss the less dramatic aspects of the faith story. Persons who had particularly powerful faith experiences can overwhelm the listener. If one speaks first of a very vivid vision or encounter with God, the friend in faith may perceive that as the model and may test every encounter against that powerful one, missing the small stirrings God places in the heart. Powerful experiences are important but need to wait until the listener can acknowledge his or her own experiences.

As important as it is to know what to say, it is also important to know what not to say. Times of separation from God are an important part of the faith story, but detailing all the aspects of one's sins is inappropriate. We are all imperfect; that message must be part of the discussion. Do not tell the deep negative parts of the past just because you are in an honest mood, especially those experiences that cannot be adequately understood or are not essential to the story. This is not the time for confession or for full disclosure or to revel in shortcomings.

It is a time to talk about faith and the events that led to that faith, and how to encounter and overcome shortcomings. In the story of Elizabeth and Sandra, Sandra was shy at first and, in the end, quite talkative, but she did not go immediately from one position to the other. For much time in the middle, Elizabeth walked the two of them through structured times. Sandra and Elizabeth's second meeting occurred a week later. Elizabeth decided that the two would meet in the park for a picnic as they talked. She wanted to talk about some of their thoughts about the church. When Sandra arrived, Elizabeth first asked about school. She knew Sandra was in the orchestra and had a public concert in two weeks. What were they playing? Were they ready? Did she like the music? Why? This helped break the ice. At first Sandra was hesitant, giving one-sentence answers. Then the conversation opened up a little.

Elizabeth steered the conversation to the mentoring program and the church. She mentioned that her first memories of their church were of recognition. Her parents took her to church and she remembered it as an important place in her family's life together. She remembered it as a friendly place where people talked to her and listened to her. She remembered it as a special place where people behaved differently. No one ran or shouted in the sanctuary. She talked about how long the sermons seemed and that she could not fully understand them. But she enjoyed the singing and the children's time with the pastor during worship. Sandra said that some of Elizabeth's experiences were like hers, but her sense of the church being important was different. She remembered church as a place that her family went on Sunday if they did not have something else planned.

From this conversation Elizabeth and Sandra talked about the church and its meaning for each of them right now. Elizabeth mentioned that the church had grown in importance in her life, especially in her later thirties. Elizabeth structured the encounter and kept the conversation going. Sandra asked questions and talked about some of her joys and frustrations with the church. Sandra opened up because Elizabeth raised the topic and kept the conversation generally on the subject. As the mentor finds ways to share faith that are genuine and timely, he or she leads in the most important way of all. (Additional guidance on sharing faith stories is given on pages 59-62, and in Appendix D, page 86.)

CREATIVITY

A good host (and mentor) *knows how to be creative.* In a mentoring relationship, *doing things together,* as well as talking about a variety of issues, is important. Conversation takes place more easily, and relationships develop more naturally when persons participate in activities together. Learning is more likely to take place with adolescents when an activity is involved.

A walk at the local mall might be a comfortable place for the mentor and the youth to talk and window-shop. Sharing such an everyday activity together eases the tension. It could also raise some issues in terms of what persons find appealing and what their attitudes are toward material possessions.

Joining in actual life experiences is a beautiful way for the mentor to speak on faith issues. Including the friend in faith on a family outing or in time spent at home with the whole family exposes the youth to the mentor's faith and how that is lived out in family life. Spending time with the mentor at work (if that is feasible), in community and service activities, and at church also offers the friend in faith the opportunity to observe how the mentor's faith influences all aspects of life and stimulates discussion around a variety of topics.

Field trips can be wonderful experiences. Spending time together at soup kitchens, hospitals, orphanages, and other church outreach locations prompts questions and discussions that lead to faith growth.

The mentor should try to schedule some of these visits, *including time for reflection together afterward*.

Another enjoyable and thought-provoking activity for mentor and youth is to rent a video or watch a TV movie together — perhaps with your family. The movie should be one that has great faith impact. Films such as "Regarding Henry," "The Karate Kid," "Awakenings," "Stanley and Iris," and "Gandhi" would be excellent discussion starters. They explore a number of caring relationships indepth and raise some significant social issues. In addition to sparking discussion, movies can also introduce subjects to the person being mentored which are new and challenging.

EMPOWERMENT

The mentoring experience is a time of *mutual empowerment*, not a one-way conversation. Both mentor and friend in faith discuss, push, and facilitate each other's growth. No one expects the mentor to have all the answers. One person's answers are not necessarily appropriate or effective for another. The mentor's role is to help the friend in faith see the answers that God gives that person. Likewise, ideally, the youth will enable the mentor to look at the answers God is offering and seek more complete understanding of those answers.

An empowerment process includes talking, reflecting, growing, and confidence, *but empowerment centers on personal confidence*. Confidence is perhaps natural to persons at birth, but our society does a lot to make people doubt their personal competence and self-worth. In the mentoring program we need to be open and accepting of persons' perceptions, and ask that they be open and accepting of our perceptions. This mutual openness and tolerance builds confidence and respect for self and for others.

Empowerment also involves *authority with responsibility*. We need authority over our beliefs and faith, authority to interact with God in ways we and God accept. Interacting with God in different ways is long-standing in the church. Peter and Paul certainly did not see eye-to-eye on all matters of faith. Each was empowered to work out a relationship with God in his own way. Empowering invests the individual with authority, yet there is a group responsibility. We must test ourselves with the group.

Empowering another involves *recognizing and affirming* that person's effective reasoning power to make decisions about matters of faith and life. In order for a person to have a mature faith, she or he must be freed from the mentor and empowered to develop faith with God directly.

LISTENING

We listen all the time, according to one definition of the word. We hear sounds and interpret what they mean. Seldom do we really hear enough of what another person is saying to understand that person. These times of insight increase as persons get to know one another better and as they practice certain listening skills. It is crucial that the mentor be a *good listener*.

One of the first criteria for listening is to create a safe environment. The mentor should listen without being judgmental. No one is willing to open up to another person in a judgmental environment.

There is a time for the mentor to talk about his or her personal journey, values, and beliefs, and what he/she feels is "right" or "wrong," but not during the listening time. Listening means opening oneself to what the other is saying in order to understand, not judge. The good mentor enables the other's thoughts to unfold and encourages the other to think and probe.

The mentor should be careful not to push the person into a belief by probing or cross-examining until he or she finds a weakness in the other person's position. This is not a court of law. The mentor is not trying to prove anything but exhibit understanding.

The mentor should listen *intently and without distraction*. Constant eye contact is important. (There is a difference between constant eye contact and staring. Staring can unnerve a person.) Remove or ignore distractions.

I know an extremely busy person who is considered by his peers to be very important and influential. He makes million-dollar decisions that dramatically affect persons' lives. But when I am in his office, I feel as if he has no other concern in the world as important as listening to me. He usually informs me how much time we have, and for that time, I have his undivided attention. Phone calls are blocked or ignored. He leaves a message that we are not to be disturbed. He never looks at the clock. He concentrates on my concern. The mentor needs to listen that attentively.

Through undivided attention and verbal reinforcement, the mentor acknowledges that the other person's words are important and valued. The mentor enhances the importance by seeking and offering feedback. The mentor may paraphrase what she or he heard in order to be clear about the meaning. The mentor offers signs and words of empathy so that the person knows that he or she is understood. The mentor affirms the person and the struggle that the person is going through, even if the mentor disagrees with the final outcome of the struggle.

The mentor should listen for what is *not* said. As the friend in faith talks, the mentor will note missing elements in what is said. These missing elements may indicate fears about those elements or fears about the potential discussion. These gaps need to be examined to enable the person to fully explore his or her faith.

Much has been written on the nonverbal. The mentor's main purpose in looking at nonverbal clues is consistency. Are the youth's nonverbal signals consistent with what he or she says? Inconsistency can mean that the trust level is low and the friend in faith is saying what he or she thinks the mentor wants to hear. It may also mean that the person has adopted one attitude on the conscious level, but subconsciously believes something quite different. Nonverbal signals may give the mentor some clues to the confusion or the intensity of the belief of the friend in faith.

CONFIDENTIALITY

Conversations must be kept confidential. Although we believe that adults can and should take care of themselves, with youth we tend to hedge on the issue of confidentiality. We often believe that we must protect the young from something, or that we owe their parents a greater responsibility than we owe the youth.

In the relationship between mentor and youth, we believe that several subjects must be reported if they come up in conversation — subjects which are as valid for adults as for youth. They are: suicide (references or inferences); child abuse (physical, sexual, or otherwise); and drug or alcohol usage. If these topics come up, the mentor should encourage the youth to seek help from a professional source. Report suspicion of child abuse to the state authorities as defined by your state law. All but two states have laws requiring this reporting. Almost all other conversations should be kept confidential. (See also the discussion of this issue in Chapter 6, pages 67-68 and 70, in relation to drug abuse and other forms of self-abuse.)

5 | STAGES

A S WITH MOST THINGS OF VALUE, mentoring requires a time commitment. It is not something one can do casually. In one sense, a mentoring relationship never ends. Some relationships are still operative years after they begin, though this is unusual. In order to be effective, plan on a minimum time commitment of three months, meeting once each week for one and a half to two hours each time.

SCHEDULES

The length of time given to the mentoring program varies from church to church. If the youth and adult are to meet once a week, the program should be at least three months long. This format is the most productive, allowing a structured time to build the relationship. One church experimented with pairing the adult and the youth once a week for one month. Though most of them met and did what was asked, the program had little impact on the participants. Evaluations indicated the following:

- Faith discussions occurred only rarely in the pairs.
- The adults and youth felt uncomfortable with one another.
- The pairs spent much of the time together in silence.
- Few wished to participate in the experience again.
- None of the relationships continued after the month was over.

Generally speaking, this one-month program was unsuccessful. Upon reflection, the design team realized they had not allowed enough time to establish relationships. The youth and the adult were still shy with each other and had not developed the trust necessary to build real relationships. The committee had shortened the program because they did not believe that youth and adults would be willing to spend three months together.

Another church experimented with a year-long program. The youth and adult met once a week for the first three months, then twice a month for the rest of the year. Most of the participants met for the first two months as agreed. After that, the participation dwindled until fewer than 50 percent were meeting when six months had passed. In the evaluations of this program the leaders discovered the following results:

- Faith discussion occurred at first but slacked off at the end.
- Adults and youth felt comfortable with one another at first, but less at ease as the program progressed.
- Active conversation was replaced by uneasiness.
- Few wished to participate in the program again.
- About 15 percent of the relationships continued for several years.

The design team, reflecting on this evaluation, decided that the program had started well, but some relationships could not sustain prolonged interaction. In a relationship that was good at first but then lost its spark, persons involved forgot about even the good.

By contrast, several congregations have participated in the format we are suggesting here. This program format calls for meetings once a week for three months. The general evaluations from these experiments have contained more positive results:

- Faith discussion occurred in 75 percent of the pairs.
- Adults and youth felt comfortable with one another and became good friends.
- Times together saw frequent animated conversations.
- Most would participate in the program again.
- About 50 percent of the relationships continued beyond the program end.

The design teams evaluated these three-month-long programs as effective in helping adults and youth talk about their faith. This is enough time to build trust and to explore basic faith issues. Faith does not happen right away, even for those who have a life-changing conversion experience. Growth in faith involves "Aha!" experiences mixed with "No, it can't be" experiences. For the mentoring program to be effective, it must exist long enough for faith discussions to be comfortable. Brief exposure to a person's faith, and then abandonment by that person, will not produce a very deep faith.

STAGES ALONG THE WAY

In discussing the time commitments of mentoring, we have already begun to think about how the mentoring relationship develops. Every relationship is, of course, unique. Nevertheless, experience has shown that healthy mentoring relationships often include certain stages of development and maturation.

In the first part of a typical relationship, the responsibility for meeting together is the mentor's. The friend in faith may not yet realize the importance of the experience or have the commitment required to be the initiator of the relationship. In the second phase of the mentoring process, the mentor and the friend in faith begin to build a level of trust and understanding. In most instances, the relationship becomes more important as it grows. In the third phase, the mentor and friend in faith discuss their own faith. They trust each other enough to discuss the issues at the core of their beliefs. Ideally, the friend in faith gains confidence as the friends grow in their faith together. Eventually, the youth may initiate meetings and open conversations. Mentors need to understand the phases of the mentoring process, remembering that each mentoring experience is different. The phases may or may not happen in the order described above.

GETTING ACQUAINTED

Sometimes the mentoring program involves groups of persons, such as confirmation classes or rites of passage groups. In these situations, whole groups of youth are invited, whether or not they are ready to enter. Peer and parent pressure push many youth into the program, though the youth do not perceive the need for a mentor.

The first meeting with the mentor and the youth together sets the tone of the relationship. Prior to this first meeting the mentor should learn everything possible about the age-level characteristics for youth. The mentor needs to understand that, as nervous as she or he is, the youth is apt to be even more so. Accept the fact, and move on with the confidence that God is always present.

At this first meeting, as we saw in the previous chapter, food usually provides a common ground. Talk and get acquainted while sharing a pizza. Set a specific beginning and ending time for the first meeting. Arrange for the youth's transportation. Parents are usually happy to provide transportation, but in some instances, they are unwilling or unable. These are the duties of the mentor as host.

Likewise, a good mentor will prepare some nonthreatening ice-breaking questions to avoid prolonged silences (see Chapter 4). These will help you get to know each other better. It is best for the adult to answer a personal question and then to ask the youth to respond, at least for the first few questions. This indicates the adult's willingness to talk and to be "put on the spot." Ask questions that require at least a sentence or two to answer — for example: "What did you do . . . ?" "How did you do . . . ?" "Why did you do . . . ?" Don't ask questions that can be answered with a simple "Yes" or "No." Remember, the purpose of this session is to get to know each other better.

When the conversation begins to move smoothly, the mentor should let it flow. Mentors should not feel that they have to ask all the questions they have prepared. The youth may take over the lead in the conversation, which is OK. The mentor directs only if the youth is over-anxious or extremely reserved. Mentors should trust their instincts. In any event, mentors should not expect to become best friends in the first meeting. Trust takes time. Depending on the youth and the mentor, their previous relationships with persons of other ages, the willingness of each to participate, and their ability to get along, trust may develop fairly quickly or may take many weeks.

Mentors should not be discouraged or compare their progress with that of other mentoring teams. Even when youth are hesitant, uncommunicative, or distant, significant progress may be taking place. The mentor may be the first adult besides family members or teachers the youth has gotten to know.

Once the trusting relationship develops, the mentor can begin slowly to share his or her own answers to some faith-related issues and ask the youth to share faith-related questions. Mentors might tell about memories of Sunday school or church. Some questions both mentor and youth could answer are:

- What is your favorite place in church?
- What does the church mean for you?
- Why do you come to church? Why do you suppose others come?
- What do you do when you are afraid? Thrilled? Worried?
- What type of person do you look for to discuss personal problems?
- What was God like for you when you were five years old?
- What is God like for you today?
- What questions do you have about God?
- What do you pray about? When do you pray?

These questions may be part of several sessions throughout the time the mentor and friend in faith are together. Again, it is helpful if some of the time the mentor speaks first and moves into deeper questions only as the time is right. Each mentor must judge when it is comfortable to move ahead or to probe deeper.

WRITING A COVENANT

Covenants have been part of the church for centuries, and part of youth involvement for decades. When local church youth go to a conference or national event, they often make covenants relating to learning goals and behavior. Many local churches also ask youth to create covenants with other youth and leaders. Covenants have the advantage of defining the event's purpose. The mentor and youth should write their covenant in the second or third meeting. It should be written at a time early in the process, yet after the initial get-acquainted time.

The value of a covenant is to provide stability when all is not perfect. When the mentoring pair are doing well, when time spent together is rewarding, meaningful, and fun, the relationship moves ahead naturally. In the hard times and in times when the mentoring pair are tempted to go in directions beyond the purpose, the covenant brings them back to the relationship.

Our relationship with God is a covenant. Membership in the church is a covenant. Marriage is a covenant. All these covenant relationships are tested, and our willingness to live up to our agreements is important during those times. We are tempted on many sides to stray from the purposes that brought us together with God, church, and other persons. In these times we can honor the covenant. Then when the bonds have been reestablished, we can let the relationship carry us on.

All covenants have a mutuality about them. They are covenants precisely because the parties involved have some say about their participation in them. With some covenants, one party writes the covenant and both parties agree to the contents. More helpful, however, are covenants written by both participants in the covenant. This provides the most complete understanding and agreement. The covenant for mentoring partners includes a third party, the church. The church has interests in the process that need to be considered and accepted.

The mentor and partner should spend at least part of one session creating a covenant to explore their purpose in being together. It is important that the church's goals are clear to both mentor and youth. An example of one church's criteria is listed below. Your design team, on behalf of your congregation, should create its own list and make a copy available to each mentoring pair.

- Meet together at least once a week for a minimum of three months.
- Be honest with each other in expressing and discussing personal faith.

- Spend time each day in prayer for your mentoring partner.
- With the exception of strictly confidential topics, discuss with your family your experience as a mentor or as a mentored youth.

The church needs to be clear with the mentoring partners whether any of the church's purposes are negotiable. When involved in a covenant, persons have the right to insist on criteria to be included. Likewise, the church, as part of the covenant, has the right to insist on the inclusion of certain criteria. The church mentioned above stresses that the items in their list are nonnegotiable, because they are important to the church's involvement in the covenant.

The mentor team should discuss the church's purposes and then add their own. They need to ask themselves, "What do I want from our time together?" Sometimes persons do not know what they want. In most instances the church and those persons asked to participate create the mentoring program. Ask youth, "What have you always wanted to know about being adult, growing up, your parents' behavior, faith, Christianity, or the church? And what do you think you need in this relationship to help you discover these things?" Ask adults, "What questions do you have about how youth can express their faith today? What agreements need to be present to enable this to happen?"

In addition to the purpose and goals of the relationship, the mentoring pair should decide what protection they need. Discussion of faith questions is confidential. What part of the conversations should remain confidential and not be discussed with parents, friends, or the pastor? Placing a confidentiality clause in a covenant makes boundaries clear. The partners should agree that the pastor must know about certain matters. Issues of suicide, abuse, or life-threatening matters should usually be brought to the pastor if they come up in discussion. Some would argue that youth will be silent on these issues if they must be reported. Most states require the reporting of suspicion of abuse. Youth need to know this. Often youth share with an adult because they want help in bringing their pain into the open. Check with your state laws to see what your obligation is.

The list is now ready to examine. The mentoring partners combine the church's expectations with theirs and write a covenant. Each partner then tells the other whether he or she can accept the covenant. If not, what in the covenant causes problems? That problem area should be rewritten or dropped. This process continues until both partners agree on a covenant. Several samples of covenants appear on the following pages.

Sample Covenant #1

For the next three months we agree to meet once each week on Wednesday at 3:00 PM (unless we select an alternative time). We further agree to discuss our time together with our families except for those things that we have agreed at the end of a session are confidential. We further agree to be honest in our discussion, reserving the right to be silent on questions. We further agree to care for and support each other with our actions and prayers.

Writing a covenant should take very little time, but it should not be taken lightly. If it takes more than one session, it wastes the partners' time together. Part of one session is usually more than adequate.

Sample Covenant #2

We, Rob and Jacob, covenant to meet once a week for the next three months. We will spend the time talking with each other about our understandings of life and faith. We will be honest and maintain in confidence all things except what we have agreed to tell our families. We will spend some of our time in recreation, prayer, and community service.

Though written in different language, each covenant example contains essentially the same ingredients. The persons involved keep their covenants for at least the three months agreed upon. The covenants serve as an external bond until the friends in faith establish an internal bond.

Sample Covenant #3

This covenant between Maria and Juanita is for a period of three months. As part of confirmation at our church, we will talk together for at least one hour each week. We will keep all of our discussions in confidence, though we will talk about what is happening with our families. We will pray for each other and support each other. We will evaluate this covenant at the end of three months.

Breaking a covenant has consequences. Few covenants are broken in a serious way; but H. Stephen Glenn indicates that it is important to establish the consequences of a broken covenant at the time the covenant is created, not after it is broken.[24] When a covenant is broken, the pair is in no position to negotiate. One possible consequence of a broken covenant might be an agreement to meet with the pastor to evaluate the relationship and to determine whether the pair can establish a new covenant. Another might be to spend a couple of weeks apart, then to meet to talk about what caused the break. Then renew the covenant or end the relationship.

> **Sample Covenant #4**
>
> We will respect each other's conversations, beliefs, and feelings. We will tell each other what is really happening in our lives. We will place a priority on our times together so only family, work, school, and church have a greater priority. We will not forsake the importance of keeping our families informed, yet we will also honor the sanctity of this relationship. We will meet for at least three months as a trial time for this relationship.

Mentors must not let relationships die of neglect. They must make decisions. If the mentoring partners are part of another program, such as confirmation, the additional goals of a long-term mentoring relationship may need to be accomplished another way. Perhaps another mentoring partnership can be established. At the very least, mentors should evaluate the relationship and seek advice from the pastor or from the design team.

SHARING FAITH EXPERIENCES

The third phase of the mentoring process is to talk about one's faith. Most people think of old-fashioned testimonies when the subject of talking about one's faith is mentioned. Testimonies have an important place in the life of a Christian, but they may suggest a kind of sharing that is restricted to certain kinds of special faith experiences — for example, conversion. Talking about faith in the context of mentoring is somewhat different. While it may include discussions of conversion or other special faith experiences, the focus is much broader. Sharing faith in this broader sense is a matter of talking about how we are working out our faith in every part of our lives. From this angle, sharing faith will often include sharing where we are struggling as well. Few of us live out our faith perfectly all of the time; most of us have a lot of growing yet to do. When mentoring partners share their faith, they share the full range of faith in the experiences of daily life.

Jesus' life and teaching indicate that God is most interested in who we are and how that flows into our everyday lives. Jesus told parables about characters who lived life in harmony with God's will and love. The story of the forgiving father (Luke 15:11ff) witnesses to love so great that even a son who squanders all is welcomed back with joy and celebration. The compassionate Samaritan (Luke 10:30ff) offers, at great expense to himself, care and concern to another. In Mark 10:14, Jesus calls on his disciples to watch his treatment of little children. In the Great Judgment (Matthew 25:32ff), the people of the nations are divided by their internal bent toward loving, caring, and helping other persons in need.

Similarly, when mentoring partners share their faith, they share where they think God is leading them in the relationships of daily life. This kind of sharing allows another person to enter your life with you, and to observe your response to life. It allows another person to ask, "Who are you really?" This can be joyful or frightening. Each of us is a witness whether or not we want to be. People enter our lives and watch us struggle with our personal temptations. The question is not whether or not witnessing will happen, but rather, will it be an intentional experience or an accidental one?

Work, play, leisure, home, church, and community are some areas of life that are part of everyday experiences. Discussing these parts of life with youth and emphasizing the importance of faith in each area will help youth experience faith more completely than will a testimony by itself.

At the same time, as we mentioned above, it is not necessary or helpful for mentors to tell everything about their lives, to "bare their souls." Mentors need to be honest, to let the friend in faith know that they are still working on some things, that they do not know all the answers, and that they too have questions. These honest admissions may open doors to exchanges that would otherwise not be possible. Remember, youth have a depth of insight and are willing to share it if we are willing to listen.

Showing our faith is not a theory, a sermon, or a verbal statement of beliefs (though each of these may be part of the process). We show faith by how we live out our beliefs in our lives. This is normal and follows the way we already do things. It requires only that we be aware of God in all that we do.

Many persons find it difficult to talk about their faith stories, often because they do not know if they have one, or they do not know the language of faith. Persons with faith stories often use words such as, "God spoke to me," "God showed me," or "God directed me." "My heart was strangely warmed, and I knew." "All of a sudden everything just fell into place." "I just knew it was the right thing." "The barriers just fell down and the doors opened." "This idea kept haunting me." "I just had to do it." These are some ways people describe how God gets involved in their lives.

God may choose special and unusual ways to speak with us. More often, God communicates through everyday happenings. Our faith is often based on how we see things. To one person the day's happenings are just happenings of the day, not God-based or God-influenced, occurring whether or not God exists. To others, the events of the day either involve God communicating directly or awaken us to our inner self where God can communicate.

Discussing faith stories is an important part of being a Christian, but do not limit stories to verbal accounts. Some are quite comfortable in the verbal arena. Others find it very difficult to talk about faith. Persons use many ways to communicate their faith stories.

One youth in a mentoring program was uncomfortable with words, but she was a very good artist. She created a series of watercolor paintings that expressed her faith. She painted the watercolors after participating in the process outlined later in this section. Her church displayed her paintings in the narthex for several Sundays. This communication of her faith was very powerful for her and for the congregation.

Another youth who found talking difficult chose song. She was a member of the church choir and often sang solos. She created a cassette tape of songs that best described her faith journey and assembled the songs in sections. One part was her inner faith journey, one her public faith journey, and another her ministry as a result of her faith journey. She chose both classical and modern songs for each area. She then wrote one song for each faith area and included them on the tape. This was a very meaningful expression of her faith. She sang her three compositions in worship one Sunday.

One person in the mentoring program of a local church had a mentally handicapping condition. He never learned to talk, though he communicated some by pointing and nodding. He could play the piano, having discovered his talent some years ago, and was moderately gifted. He chose to express his faith in a piano selection that he composed and played for the congregation. The piece was moving and many said that they sensed his struggle as well as a deep peace.

The three youth above chose the ways they knew best to express their faith stories. In this world persons often choose to express faith in action, art, and meditation, as well as in words. Each person in the mentoring program should tell his or her faith story publicly at some time in some way. If the youth are in a confirmation program, they can do this just before they complete the program. The mentor helps and encourages the youth to discover and work on a personal story. (Additional help in the preparation of faith stories can be found in Appendix D, page 86.)

DOING FAITH AND MINISTRY

As we saw in the description of various historical models of mentoring (Chapter 1), persons can learn a trade by working with a mentor. This involves more than watching and talking about the trade or profession. It involves practicing the trade under the watchful eyes of the mentor. We have drifted away from the "doing" aspect of teaching. Most of what we teach is mind learning. Yet faith has strong action components. Just consider the following passage from the New Testament account of Jesus' teaching.

When the Son of Man comes in his glory, and all the angels with him, then he will sit on the throne of his glory. All the nations will be gathered before him, and he will separate people one from another as a shepherd separates the sheep from the goats, and he will put the sheep at his right hand and the goats at the left. Then the king will say to those at his right hand, "Come, you that are blessed by my Father, inherit the kingdom prepared for you from the foundation of the world; for I was hungry and you gave me food, I was thirsty and you gave me something to drink, I was a stranger and you welcomed me, I was naked and you gave me clothing, I was sick and you took care of me, I was in prison and you visited me." Then the righteous will answer him, "Lord, when was it that we saw you hungry and gave you food, or thirsty and gave you something to drink? And when was it that we saw you a stranger and welcomed you, or naked and gave you clothing? And when was it that we saw you sick or in prison and visited you?" And the king will answer them, "Truly I tell you, just as you did it to one of the least of these who are members of my family, you did it to me" (Matthew 25:31-40).

Could anything be clearer? Faith is important, yet living out that faith in everyday life is also important. In order to offer the most comprehensive mentoring process, mentors need to involve their friends in faith in acts of concrete ministry. There are many ways to do this.

One helpful involvement in ministry is for the mentor to invite the friend in faith to be part of a ministry in which the mentor is already involved (if this is practical). Starting a new ministry as a team can also be effective. Following are a few suggestions about ministries that youth and adults can do together.

 ␻ ***Worship Ministry to the Homebound***. Many churches tape their worship services and someone from the church takes the tape to persons unable to attend the service. Some youth and adults have made this project their responsibility, but they have done it in ways that went beyond just delivering a tape. An example is Fred and Andy. After church each Sunday they prepared a meal for the homebound person and themselves. They took the meal to the person's house and ate together, starting the meal with grace. During the meal, Fred and Andy related to the person the events and feeling of the worship service. They talked about the hymns, the scripture, and the sermon. They discussed concerns and joys that people had. They described the flowers on the altar.

    Fred took the lead in the early meetings with the homebound. As the relationship built and Andy became more comfortable with the process, Fred encouraged Andy to talk more and more. After several meetings Andy led almost all the time together. Finally Fred encouraged Andy to meet with the homebound person alone. This ministry enabled that person to experience the worship service in a way that merely listening to the tape could not. It also helped the friend in faith grow in faith and understanding.

 ␻ ***Food Kitchen***. Some mentors involve their friends in faith in a food kitchen, volunteering to help with one meal a week. Help includes preparing and serving the meal, and talking about God and life issues with the persons who come for food.

    Initially, the youth may simply sit and listen or occasionally stir a pot. But as time passes, the youth will take on more and more responsibility, including cooking and serving. The opportunity to listen to and to talk with those who come to eat also increases. The youth and mentor complete the sessions with discussions about feeding the hungry.

 ␻ ***Ministry with Persons with Handicapping Conditions***. Amy (the mentor) and Jill (the youth) were aware of the city's horseback riding program for differently-abled persons. Jill indicated a real joy in riding and being around horses, so the two volunteered to help with the program. They went together and learned together. They helped groom and feed the horses, and helped persons with mentally handicapping conditions ride the horses. They committed a half-day a week to this work. Amy and Jill were instrumental in helping the program involve the participants in feeding and grooming the horses as well as riding. They also talked with the persons about horses and about life.

☙ *Children's Hospital.* One group of mentors and youth worked in the local hospital's children's ward. Each day right after school one mentor and youth went to the hospital to tell the children stories. Some children's parents cannot visit frequently or stay for long periods of time at the hospital. The storytelling teams take some of this burden off the parents, and let these children know that other people care for them and love them very much. The mentors assumed initial responsibility for preparing stories. As time progressed, the friends in faith took more and more responsibility. They began to prepare the stories, taking the initiative for creative storytelling. Eventually the mentor sometimes let the youth assume all responsibility in the children's ward.

☙ *Workcamp.* Some mentors and youth choose a more concentrated time to be in ministry. A workcamp involves going to a location for a week or two to help people in need. The help often involves repairing or building, combined with a relationship to the persons being helped. The best workcamps usually involve some reciprocal giving. In one such camp, mentors and youth repaired and painted the siding on the home of persons who could not do the work themselves or afford to pay someone for the repairs. The people in the home gave woodcarving lessons to the mentors and youth. They also all worshiped and had Bible study together each day. The mentors took control of the work at the beginning. They also planned the first worship and Bible study. However, as the week progressed, the youth assumed responsibility for more and more of the work, worship, and Bible study. In this way, the mentors showed the friends in faith what they were capable of accomplishing.

Many other possibilities for ministry exist in your community. The important point is that *persons learn by doing.* Doing provides confidence and a feeling for what living the faith is really like. Christianity is a doing and feeling religion.

PHYSICAL SETTINGS FOR MENTORING

Before we leave the subject of stages of mentoring, we should also comment on how the development of the relationship can influence the location of meetings. Mentoring can occur anywhere. Most sessions take place in the adult's normal life space, because the youth is observing the adult and the way he or she integrates Christianity with his or her life. In the broadest sense, mentoring occurs whenever and wherever the youth sees or hears anything involving his or her mentor. All of life is a part of the mentoring process. The youth and adult do not turn observations on and off. It is easier to discuss spiritual formation at the moment of the observations.

Nevertheless, as we have already stated, in the early stages of mentoring, neutral or safe places are most comfortable to both persons. Jack's and Henry's first meetings (Chapter 1) took place in a pizza parlor, as did Elizabeth's and Sandra's (Chapter 4). This kind of location provides safety in several ways. It is a public place frequented by youth and adults, a place not usually known for intense discussion, a place of fun and fellowship, and a place of the community. It is easy to feel comfortable in such a setting.

As the mentoring process continues, the youth and adult will probably want to meet at more significant places, such as at each other's homes, at a workplace, at school, or at the church building. The realities of life the partners wish to explore will help determine the location. All meetings should take place, however, in a way that is open to observation by others and does not invite reproach.

Long-Range Interaction?

After the initial period of scheduled meetings (we suggest three months of weekly meetings), the mentoring partners should be able to determine the frequency of future interaction. Some will decide to stop meeting on a regular basis. They may speak at church or other places they may happen to meet, but the intentional meetings are over. Others continue to meet less frequently, or they may exchange phone calls and letters. Both partners must determine what is comfortable and helpful for them.

A rest time may follow the intensity of the initial three months. Contact by the mentor after a couple of months is often welcome and helpful. Persons need an inactive time to regroup. Then it is easier to renew the relationship in a comfortable form.

People who are important to others cannot just leave them. If a mentor spends significant time with a youth and then later acts as if the youth doesn't exist, this may be worse than not having a mentor at all. Experience shows that a mentoring program will be unsuccessful if the participating adults see their roles as short-term. When adults merely "do their time," then go back to ignoring the youth with whom they have been in significant conversation, the youth feel that adults do not really care for them. The sense of failed friendship casts doubt on the sincerity of all the discussions the two had. People who are really important to others take the time to care — even after the program is over.

6 | QUESTIONS

THE DESCRIPTIONS WE HAVE GIVEN of the mentoring program will no doubt raise many questions. This chapter is an attempt to anticipate some of these and to offer some brief responses. This, in turn, should help pastors and other leaders in the task of presenting the mentoring program to their congregation. You might even consider using these questions in a discussion setting in order to encourage people to ask their own questions. The following questions are organized according to the identities of the persons most likely to ask them: youth, parents, and potential mentors.

QUESTIONS OF YOUTH

1. *"What do I say?"* This is typically one of the first questions youth ask. It suggests a good deal of anxiety. Youth and adults do not communicate much in this country. Often when they get together there is silence. They just do not know what to say. The world views of many youth are very different from those of many adults. Freda Gardner talks of adults who work with youth in the church, "What world view, lifestyles, major questions, values, hopes and goals marked the lives of these adults as they struggled with identity, sex, occupation, friendship, ideologies? What language, humor, music, recreation, idols, literature shaped their dream and despair and dictated their choices? These women and men — the parents, teachers, pastors, club and group leaders, policy-makers — were born in the late 30's and early 40's to World War I and Great Depression-oriented parents. Things are different from when you were kids."[25] So youth and adults often find no common ground for starting a discussion. As a result, youth and adults seldom talk.

In other words, youth have a legitimate concern. The most important answer, however, is not really an answer; it is an action that adults can take — creative listening. Even though world views and feelings may be very different, underlying growth problems are the same. Youth and adults find much to talk about when they take time to listen.

2. *"Will I be asked a lot of questions?"* Youth worry that adults will ask them questions about the Bible or religion. School comprises a large part of youth's involvement with adults, and school is in a question-and-answer format. Likewise, youth's church relationship with adults is usually in the church school context, where youth are asked a lot of questions. The adults' questions may be about the church or about life, but they are still questions with right or wrong answers. Understandably, youth are hesitant to enter into another relationship where this is the basic expectation.

Even when youth are assured that mentoring is not a class setting, they believe the process is made up of questions. If mentoring is part of a confirmation setting, this suspicion may be even greater. Actually talking with a mentor will dispel this idea. After the youth and adult spend several meetings together, the expectations change.

3. *"Will what I say to my mentor be shared with others?"* This question points to the importance of confidentiality, a very real concern that we dealt with in Chapter 2 (as a benefit of mentoring to youth) and in Chapter 4 (as a skill of the mentor). Typically, youth are reluctant to tell an adult about really important personal "stuff." If adults want to provide a safe place for youth to share their questions and problems, the adults must know how to keep confidences.

In most cases, mentors will find that the value of their relationships with youth only increases as they share and keep confidences. As the level of trust in the relationship increases, youth will open up and will want to share their questions and problems. As mentioned previously, these may be questions related to common teenage problems, such as how to get along with parents; or they may relate to other kinds of personal problems, such as how to accept the physical, emotional, and sexual changes they are experiencing. Most of the time, this kind of sharing will not raise an issue of moral accountability for the welfare of the youth on the part of the adult mentor. While the adult may not approve all of the ways in which the youth is approaching a question or problem, the best way to help will be to continue serving as sounding board, a safe place to share. Some cases, however, can raise questions of moral accountability. Just consider what happened to Sally.

Sally spent a lot of time at her friend's house. They were almost inseparable. Because of this, after several months, Sally got to know her friend's mother quite well. She enjoyed talking with her "second mom," almost as much as with her friend. She began to trust her, confiding in her more and more. Since Sally's friend's mom smoked, Sally mentioned that several of her friends smoked and that she occasionally joined them. Sally was surprised later when she got home and was confronted by her mother, who accused her of smoking, asked for reasons, and grounded her. Sally asked her mother where she had heard this. Her friend's mother had called just before Sally got home. Sally felt angry, disillusioned, and betrayed. She had liked and trusted her friend's mother, and now she felt that she could never tell her anything again. Adults often repeat to parents and other adults what youth say to them. The result is that youth are afraid to talk to adults, assuming they will violate the confidentiality of their discussions.

Sally's story illustrates a difficult situation that can arise in the mentor/partner relationship. Should a mentor report an experiment with smoking to pastor or parents? What about an experiment with drugs? Or sex? These questions raise others. Does the mentor know for sure that the behavior is taking place? How old is the youth — pre-teen or late teen? Will a direct report to parent or guardian subject the youth to a known pattern of child abuse? In Sally's case the report seemed to be valid, since Sally herself made the admission; yet her behavior was only a matter of an experiment with smoking. In this particular case, the mentor might have fairly concluded that Sally was not sufficiently endangering herself to warrant breaking confidence and potentially ending the mentor relationship. On the other hand, if the behavior were of a more serious nature, the mentor would be under greater moral obligation to care for Sally precisely by risking the future of their relationship.

There are no hard and fast rules that determine precisely what to do in every case. In each case, mentors must weigh the value of maintaining confidences, providing a place where youth can raise questions and "confess" problems, against the potential of abuse — even self-abuse. Just as mentors have a responsibility under the law to report incidences of suspected child abuse to the proper legal authorities, so they have a moral responsibility to youth and to parents to report incidences of serious self-abuse. If parental relationships are already shaky, the mentor should seek the advice of the pastor in how to proceed. The mentor should make every effort as well to encourage the youth to seek professional help. In any event, the pain of breaking confidences must be weighed against the harm of allowing the behavior to continue. The youth may eventually thank the mentor for caring enough to tell, but the youth may also turn away and refuse further contact. Keeping confidence is a great responsibility. If the mentor determines that confidence must be broken, then the pastor should be notified and the youth informed.

4. *"Will this adult really care about me?"* Another concern for most youth is acceptance. They fear that adults do not really accept them. Because the mentoring program is set up for youth to choose adults, there is some risk that the adult will not make the same choice. The youth do not usually know that most adults feel honored to be chosen and look forward to the experience.

One friend in faith exhibited inattentive and sometimes rude behavior during meetings. He was constantly disruptive, rapping his pencil while his mentor talked. In the middle of conversations he got up to look out the window, or left the room in the middle of a sentence, and was in general very restless. The mentor had looked forward to this time, but was now feeling ineffective. He told the pastor of the youth's behavior, asking what he could do.

The pastor suggested that the mentor confront the youth directly and ask what the youth was trying to say. The mentor spoke to the youth, saying that he was confused and wanted to know what the youth's behavior meant. At first the youth avoided the question, but finally admitted he had been testing his mentor. The youth did not think that the adult would accept him, and wanted to see how much his mentor would put up with before he ended the relationship. Once the air cleared and the youth felt accepted, the discussion warmed and they talked about significant topics.

Though most youth do not act out as negatively as the youth in this example, they are looking for adults who will listen and accept them as persons, even when they disagree on a subject. Youth often set up a barrier to communication with others. They are quiet until they feel someone will listen. If no one appears to listen, they believe they are not personally accepted, and, of course, will not make an effort to share thoughts and feelings. Adults who are aware of this type of behavior can work early on at breaking the ice by listening and demonstrating that they accept youth even during disagreements.

Most youth will eventually find having a mentor to be of great benefit to them. Unfortunately, they discover these benefits *as the program unfolds and as they participate in it*. The "pluses" of the program may not be obvious to youth at the outset. Orientation and involvement of youth quickly after choosing the mentors will help dispel misgivings about the program.

QUESTIONS OF PARENTS

1. *"Is my child ready for a relationship with another adult?"* Some parents have trouble dealing with the inclusion of another significant adult in the lives of their youth. Parents sometimes find it difficult to let go. Again, adolescence is a time of change. Parents are not always willing to admit that youth are no longer children but need to be viewed as emerging adults. When parents do not recognize this emergence, they tend to restrict opportunities for youth to make decisions, holding back their children. Sometimes it is a reluctance to give up childhood; sometimes they simply do not realize that the youth are ready to begin making responsible decisions on their own.

2. *"Will a mentoring relationship make my role as parent less important?"* Occasionally parents are jealous (consciously or unconsciously) of their youth's new relationship with another adult. Parents may be reluctant to see their youth talking, laughing, and opening up to someone other than themselves, especially if the parental relationship is stormy. Parents may be concerned and wonder why this noncommunicative person who lives in their house suddenly turns into a bright, bubbling conversationalist with someone else. Most realize that they really are good parents and are not doing anything wrong. Such behavior just goes with the territory of living with youth. (See also the discussion of the benefit to parents of the mentoring relationship, pages 14-18.)

Sherry's mother felt some of those pangs when she saw Sherry and Donna together. Sherry was deep in the stage of being critical of everything her mother did, said, or wore. Although Sherry's mother was aware that Sherry was going through a stage, it was sometimes disconcerting. Fortunately she realized that Donna was not taking over her role as parent, but simply providing Sherry with another supportive adult relationship.

3. *"Will the mentoring relationship break the confidences of our family life?"* If the mentor relationship gets to be particularly close, parents may worry about what family information is being shared. Youth often divulge all sorts of family stories that parents wish they would keep confidential within the family. This is a risk all parents must face. They no longer have total control over what youth say and to whom. This is part of letting go. Naturally, mentors will keep family information in the same confidence that they keep other information provided by youth.

4. *"Will the mentor set a good example for my teenager?"* Parents may be concerned about the new adult's cultural influence on their youth. If the relationship gets close, the influence will be significant. Parents need to be aware of this possibility. A mentor's lifestyle and personal taste may be somewhat different from that of the parents, and youth may choose to emulate their mentors in certain ways. Parents cannot shield them from the influence of others. Parents must trust that the major underlying values they have lived and instilled in their children will remain unchanged.

5. *"Will my child be physically and morally safe with the mentor?"* The issue of physical safety needs to be addressed. Parents are allowing their youth to spend special time with this new adult. They need some knowledge of the mentor and his or her habits. Is this person a safe driver? Can this person be trusted to use proper moral conduct around the youth, such as refraining from using inappropriate language?

Concerns about physical safety and other basic values are usually alleviated by the fact that this program originates in the church and therefore has certain built-in safeguards. The process of pairing youth and mentor is handled by the pastor(s), who usually knows or can gather needed information about persons in the congregation. If any question arises about the persons selected for mentors, the pastor must make inquiries and find out all that he or she can about these persons prior to allowing them to become mentors. (See also the discussion of child abuse issues on pages 40-41.)

6. *"Does my child have time for this kind of relationship?"* Some parents at first object to their youth's involvement in ministry programs. Youth's lives are already so busy with school, sports, music lessons, and clubs, there seems to be no time for ministry programs. But everyone must look at priorities. An individual's spiritual development is as important as the physical, intellectual, aesthetic, and social. Youth should spend a proportionate amount of time on the spiritual. Other activities may have to be cut back in order to spend time in ministry.

QUESTIONS OF MENTORS

Persons selected as mentors also have questions and concerns. This is natural, since mentoring is an awesome responsibility. The concerns of adult mentors regarding a mentoring program are many and varied. Some are similar to the questions of youth and parents. Not all adults will raise the same questions. In order to present a total picture, however, some of these questions need to be examined.

1. *"Do I have time for this?"* Once an adult has said "yes" and has gotten used to the initial honor of being asked to serve, he or she may have second thoughts about the time commitment required. At this point, the adult needs to be reassured that the mentoring relationship can be tailored to meet personal needs. The actual schedule for meeting is something that will be worked out between the mentor and the friend in faith. Some mentors find that they have lots of time to spend. In other cases, time is limited and must be used wisely. Some find time to go out to lunch, ball games, movies, and the like. The time commitment should be mutually acceptable to both the mentor and the friend in faith. Time together needs to deal with getting to know each other and building a relationship that allows for trust, revelation, and mutual growth.

2. *"What will be expected of me?"* To summarize what we saw in Chapters 3, 4, and 5, we may say that the main expectation of the mentor is to provide a place where he or she can explore faith issues with the youth. The depth to which this happens depends entirely on the "fit" of the two persons involved. Sometimes it is a natural fit and the persons involved form a deep, long-lasting relationship. Other times the experience lasts no longer than the time involved in the confirmation process. No one can predict exactly what will happen. Any time spent getting to know each other is a plus for both parties concerned.

3. *"What will I say?"* As with youth, this is one of the biggest questions in the minds of adults. Of course there is no way to create a script for the mentoring relationship. Indeed, if we think about it, none of us would really want a script for a relationship in which we are supposedly trying to develop openness, mutual care, and spiritual candor. Nevertheless, it may be helpful to recall the principle of moving from lesser to greater in matters of sharing. For example, in Chapters 4 and 5, we provided some models of ice-breaking questions. These questions are designed to get participants talking. The questions have been carefully thought out to begin at a nonthreatening level and to provide common ground for dialogue. When two persons of differing backgrounds, ages, and interests

form a relationship, they need to establish a common area from which to begin. The principle of moving from simple to more profound issues is a good one to follow in most cases.

4. *"Suppose I don't know the answer?"* This is the flip-side of the youth concern that adult mentors will ask questions that require right or wrong answers. As adults we often feel that we are supposed to know certain things and will be seen as inferior or even incompetent if we do not. Youth do not really expect us to know everything. Indeed, youth have much more respect for someone who is willing to admit to not having all the answers. The big mistake is to try to fake it. Children and youth have a remarkable way of seeing through pretense. They have far more respect for the answer, "I really don't know. Let's see if we can find out together," than for a pat answer that they may later discover is wrong.

5. *"Will I be accepted?"* Concern about acceptance does not go away as we grow taller and older. In most cases the friend in faith has selected the mentor based on some knowledge, instinct, or preconceived notion. Therefore most teams already have some basis for a relationship. If a choice has been made for the youth, this scenario may change. Usually, responsible adults can find grounds for a relationship. We can give as much of ourselves as is possible and pray that our presence has made a difference in some way. Not every mentoring pair will become lifelong friends. We may touch a life in some way and never know just what an impact we make. Few mentoring relationships are complete failures.

6. *"Will a youth really be able to understand my adult experience of faith?"* Once again, the quality of the relationship will best determine the answer to this question. If conversation is open, honest, and appropriate, the answer is most likely "yes." Youth are far more astute than we sometimes realize. They will sort out what we discuss with them and make a decision based on their level of maturity and understanding.

When Betsy told her friend in faith, Stacey, about her anger toward God when her child was born with handicapping conditions, Stacey could understand why Betsy was angry. She would have been surprised at most other responses. Betsy went on to say that her faith in a caring God was the only thing that made life possible for awhile, and that was the message that came through to Stacey. Youth are perceptive and understanding.

APPENDIX A
Planner's Workshop

One of the first steps in planning is for the pastor and design team to achieve clarity about how the mentoring program can fit into the other areas of ongoing ministry in the congregation. To this end, the team needs to clarify in its own mind at least two major points: the *basic meaning and form of a mentoring relationship*, and the *best way(s) to use this form of ministry* in the congregation. Below is a workshop agenda that can help the team work through these issues in an orderly way.

This workshop may also be used in conjunction with a presentation to the decision-making board or council of the congregation. In this way the council will be included in the earliest stages of prayer and planning. The workshop may also be adapted for use in presenting the concept of mentoring to the entire congregation. This is only a sample workshop. It can be altered by your committee to present the "big picture" of what mentoring is and how it might be incorporated for the benefit of your congregation.

Workshop Agenda

1. Synonyms for Mentoring *(5 min.)*

2. A Basic Definition *(5 min.)*

3. Models of Mentoring *(10 min.)*

4. Personal Stories *(10 min.)*

5. Possibilities in Our Church *(20 min.)*

6. Focusing the Possibilities *(10 min.)*

---

1. Print the word **mentor** on a sheet of newsprint. As persons enter, ask them to write synonyms for this term on the newsprint. Some possibilities: **teacher, counselor, friend, consultant, sponsor, coach, supporter, guide, facilitator, advisor, enabler.**

2. Print a definition: "**Mentor:** a close, trusted, and experienced counselor or guide," and "teacher, tutor, coach."[26] Along with this definition, explain that the mentoring concept has captured the imagination of a wide range of individuals and groups. It is being used in business, industry, social services, education, and health fields, among others. The mentor relationship was present in the early church. Persons who had confessed faith in God and Christ were shepherded by the community for as long as two years before they were baptized. Mentoring helped each person develop his or her spiritual gifts. Galatians 6:1 asks Christians to "restore . . . in a spirit of gentleness." James 5:16 says, "Confess your sins to one another, and pray for one another, so that you may be healed." The church community was concerned one for the other. Persons who had walked the same path before cared for and helped those beginning their spiritual journeys.

3. As leader, list some notable models of mentoring relationships, and ask persons to discuss why these relationships have played such an important role. Start with the origin of the term **mentor** in the story of Ulysses (see Chapter 1, pages 1-2). Proceed to discuss some of the other historical, biblical, and ecclesial models as presented in Chapter 1.

   - Carpenter and Apprentice
   - Jesus and Peter
   - The Irish Soul Friend
   - Doctor and Intern
   - Paul and Timothy
   - Ruth and Naomi
   - The United Methodist ritual of baptism

4. Now invite participants to share personal experiences in which they have benefited from the example of a mentor. Who was that mentor? What were the circumstances, results, and feelings that participants remember from their relationships?

5. Next, invite the participants to explore some specific ways your congregation might adapt mentoring for your ministry. Ask

participants to list groups of people in the ministry area of your congregation who might benefit from a mentoring program. Encourage them to name specific ways the congregation might make mentoring a part of the whole church philosophy. (This includes youth in general, youth in groups, confirmation classes, membership classes, profession of faith classes, teacher training, leader training, etc.; see Appendix B: Mentoring Possibilities, page 77.) Add to the list as many ways as you can think of to use the ministry of mentoring.

6. As a final step, develop some criteria for selecting the best and most usable ideas from the list the group generated. Of the ways listed, ask the group to select which would be most beneficial to your congregation and to the persons you want to serve. Some criteria to follow are:

- Which persons most need a mentoring experience?
- Which persons does our church not now reach with significant ministry?
- Which persons could we reach first because of mechanisms already in place?
- Which persons can we reach because the church has already expressed concern about this group of people?

Close the workshop by inviting the participants to determine their interest level in the mentoring program by indicating how much energy they personally are willing to invest. Are they excited and willing to tell their stories and invite other persons into the process?

APPENDIX B
Mentoring Possibilities

As persons come to understand the basic concept of mentoring, they usually begin to think of ways mentoring can be helpful in other ministries of their congregation. Indeed, as mentioned in Chapter 3, and in Appendix A, this is one of the first steps your design team will want to take in organizing a mentoring program. Even after an initial program is successfully completed, moreover, creative minds will continue to think: "How else might we use this concept? Where else is a mentoring relationship a natural extension of our caring process?" This appendix is designed to help you imagine a number of possibilities and to keep the way open for the future.

1. *How can the mentoring program be organized so its benefits are available to all new church members?* It is always difficult for people who are new to a congregation to become truly incorporated. The problem is not solved simply by taking the big step of joining. The really crucial steps are all of the little things that have to happen if new people are truly to become part of the fellowship. Mentoring is a wonderful way for the church to help new people find their places of fellowship, nurture, and service in the congregation!

Consider the story of Mary and Sam. Mary and Sam moved to town and began church shopping. Their first visit to one congregation was followed by a letter and a visit from the pastor. They soon decided to join this congregation and were assigned a family unit who would serve as their mentors. Betty and Jim, who had a young child and were active in the church and community, agreed to become mentors for this young couple. Mary was pregnant, and while her previous doctor had referred her to a new doctor, she still had many things to learn. Betty introduced Mary to her pediatrician and to the new parents' class at church, supplied her with a list of reliable babysitters, and told her where the best dry cleaner was. Betty also brought Mary to her church women's group and introduced her to other women in the church. Betty was very helpful in smoothing out the rough spots in Mary's transition.

Mary was feeling lonely and alone. She and Sam had each other, and that relationship was good. But she knew almost no one else. She found a friend and confidant in Betty. They started out talking about things important to persons new in a community and progressed to talking about faith issues and how to live their faith in everyday life. They helped each other grow and work through their doubts. As their relationship grew, they found a closeness beneficial to both of them; they helped each other to grow in faith. Initially Betty served as mentor to Mary, but as the relationship grew, they helped each other. Later their relationship broadened to include their families.

Sam found Jim very helpful, and they became friends as well. Jim invited Sam to his local service club and introduced Sam to persons active in the business community. Sam went along with Jim on the church-sponsored "Habitat for Humanity" day and found a way to use his love for repairing things in a way that provided a much-needed community service. Sam met other men of the church through Jim and joined a men's Bible study group. The Bible study challenged Sam, and he and Jim often discussed their faith as it was informed by their class. The discussions most often included Mary and Betty, as the two couples spent much of their free time together.

The mentoring relationship the church provided for this new family was helpful in countless ways. It provided them assistance for the transition after their move. It helped Mary and Sam get involved in activities and become part of the church community. It provided a much-needed caring unit for these young persons in a new environment. This mentoring happened because the church was prepared to accept persons as their responsibility.

2. *What are some other ways we might use mentoring in the youth program?* The senior high youth group in one congregation was very strong and very close. New persons coming into this program had difficulty becoming part of the group. The group was so close-knit that it automatically preferred the companionship of persons already in the group, and after an initial welcome tended to ignore new arrivals. The group decided to try a mentoring approach to determine if this would make the atmosphere more open. Each new person in the youth group was assigned to an established member. The youth were prepared to think differently. They accepted shepherding new youth as their responsibility. This made a big difference to new youth like Mindy.

Mindy was popular and active in the church's junior high youth group. She looked forward to moving into the senior high group, but had heard and was concerned that it was a clique. Sandra, a high school sophomore, was assigned to be Mindy's shepherd, or mentor. Sandra phoned Mindy two weeks before the first senior high meeting and invited her to come, offering to pick Mindy up and bring her to the meeting. Sandra explained a bit about the youth group's activities and told Mindy what to expect for the coming year.

Mindy was thrilled with the personal invitation and welcomed the idea of walking into that first meeting with someone. She found it helpful to know what kinds of things the group was involved in, and decided she couldn't wait to help the girls' team collect the most food for the youth group's annual food drive.

Mindy was entering her freshman year at Sandra's high school. The girls talked about that as well. Sandra agreed to meet Mindy at school and show her around. Mindy was grateful for Sandra's advice about the ins and outs of her new school, and learned who to talk to about trying out for the track team. Mindy found Sandra a help and comfort at a new and somewhat apprehensive time in her life. Sandra discovered that it was fun to play guide, and that she liked being able to impart some of her knowledge and experience.

Sandra and Mindy kept their relationship at a nonspiritual level for a while. Eventually they confided in each other some concerns, doubts, and beliefs about faith matters. When two persons talk regularly, spiritual matters usually come into the discussion. Subjects that come up in youth group can be dealt with in other conversations. The spiritual mentoring, though less formal than in some programs, still happens.

3. *How can we use mentoring in the process of training teachers for the church school setting?* One of the perennial tasks of Christian education programs is teacher training. In far too many cases, however, teacher training tends to be perfunctory, telling potential candidates little that they did not already know, or giving them little information that will really help them over the course of a full season of teaching. Mentoring can provide the kind of personal interaction that brings spiritual depth back to the process of teacher training.

When Carla agreed to become a teacher in the church school program of her congregation, she had no training and lacked confidence in her classroom skills. Instead of putting Carla through a brief introductory course in teaching, the director of Christian education decided to use a mentoring process. The director placed Carla with Pam, a certified public school teacher who had also taught the first grade church school for ten years. Pam was an effective teacher, and Carla agreed to be her apprentice, co-teaching with Pam.

After two years teaching side by side with Pam, Carla felt she was ready to teach her own class. She had helped plan and teach lessons, set the climate for the room, engaged the students in discussion, and acquired teaching skills to the point where she was confident and self-assured. Pam then served as a mentor for Ellen, and has gone on to enable other persons to become confident enough to teach on their own. Pam is a master at teaching her knowledge and skills and at training persons to perform on their own.

Pam was also a mentor on the spiritual level. Both her actions and her knowledge were open for her friends in faith to see. In preparing for the lessons, Pam emphasized the importance of being personally spiritually prepared to teach. Teaching involves more than techniques or knowing what to do when. It is a way of life. Each teacher is a role model for the students. Pam was tuned in to the importance of this spiritual preparation. She confronted the friends in faith for whom she was mentor, helping them grow in their relationship with God. She helped persons strengthen their prayer life and make their faith more a part of their behavior.

4. *Many other possibilities exist for using mentoring effectively in the church.* Look at the big picture and remember that the focus of mentoring is to help persons develop and grow. Just consider briefly a few of the following:

- How might we use mentoring *to help older youth and college students explore a specific direction of career planning?* Think of the benefits of a youth observing a person work in his or her chosen field, struggling with what it means to be a Christian in the workplace.

- How can we use mentoring *to reach out to youth in the community who are at risk?* When Jesus walked the pathways of this earth, he was often among the sinners and outcasts of the world. Mentoring relationships with caring adults provide a way to help youth who are trying to resist drugs, alcohol, and violence. The number of youth at risk is high, within as well as outside of the church. The church could reach out to youth who have been abused, are in trouble sexually, or are at the edge of suicide.

- Could our congregation provide a mentoring program that *effectively reaches out to every youth in the church?* What if the mentor and friend in faith could be together for the whole junior high and senior high experience? What if this relationship carried on through college years? Think of the benefits to each person involved!

Mentoring allows us all to grow by sharing the faith we live with others. The possibilities for mentoring in the church are limitless. Creative minds just need to keep thinking and asking questions.

APPENDIX C
Participant's Workshop

Invite all interested youth, their parents, and some potential mentor candidates to an informal gathering. The purpose of this gathering is to introduce the concept and vision for mentoring to this group of potential participants and to begin to build a sense of rapport among the parents, youth, and mentors. If the mentoring program is to work, persons need to trust one another, be honest with one another, and keep necessary confidences.

In Chapter 3 (pages 31-33) we discussed how youth should be included in the process of naming and selecting mentors. The nominating process can take place either prior to this workshop or after it. If mentors are nominated before the workshop, then all of the candidates the youth name should be invited to participate in the workshop. On the other hand, the pastor and design team might also use the workshop as an opportunity to introduce spiritually mature adults to youth who have not met one another before. In this case, the design team invites a group of potential mentors to the workshop, and the youth use the workshop experience to inform their selection of nominees. Of course, the two approaches may also be blended.

In any case, it is a good idea to center this gathering around a meal or snack, such as a continental breakfast, a light lunch, pizza, or dessert. This setting helps create an informal atmosphere. Invite individuals to the gathering by card or letter, with follow-up phone calls. (In some instances, the family of specific youth are not able or willing to attend, especially youth who come from non-church families. Provide these youth with adult sponsors, persons from the church who have been instrumental in their lives. The sponsors may be teachers, youth advisors, or parents of friends. It is important that the youth have some adult support in addition to the mentor candidates at this meeting.)

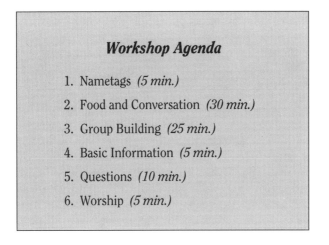

Workshop Agenda

1. Nametags *(5 min.)*
2. Food and Conversation *(30 min.)*
3. Group Building *(25 min.)*
4. Basic Information *(5 min.)*
5. Questions *(10 min.)*
6. Worship *(5 min.)*

1. As persons gather, ask each to make a nametag. In many churches not all participants will know one another. This starts everyone off with the same advantage and also gives persons something to do as they arrive. In smaller churches, however, where everyone knows each other because they have lived in the same community and attended the same church all their lives, nametags may be not only superfluous but offensive.

2. After making nametags, take time to enjoy food and conversation together. Enhance the opportunity for conversation by providing smaller tables (such as card tables), rather than the long ones most churches have. Two card tables together accommodate six, which makes a good conversation group. It is helpful to have families sit together at a table with another family or a mentor.

3. Schedule a group-building experience next on the agenda. Group building is an important part of the process, providing a foundation for a relationship that will be important to each person. It helps build a relationship between youth and adults other than their parents. Parents will feel more comfortable as they learn something about the mentors. It usually makes the ensuing meetings easier. Here is one exercise that has worked well in other congregations:

- Place one youth, his or her parents, and a mentor together. The group answers several nonthreatening questions that elicit name, place of birth, last movie seen in a theater, favorite food, hobbies, or favorite leisure activity. These are relatively non-intrusive and apply to all ages. The questions also provide background about the people.

- After the initial questions, let persons begin telling faith stories. On a sheet of paper, each person writes down his or her earliest memories of God. What was God like? What did God do? On the other side of the paper, the person answers the questions as he or she now perceives God. A person may write two sets of words or phrases on each side of the paper. The first set is what the person actually remembers or believes. The second set is what the person thinks he or she is supposed to believe. Give persons time to add to the first side of their papers. What are the first memories of God? Tell the group that there is no wrong answer to the question, because God is bigger than any of our concepts. We may not all see the same part of God.

- When all finish, ask volunteers to discuss the similarities and differences in these memories, and to speculate on what influenced their early conceptions. The group can then discuss the second side of the sheet of paper.

- Give each person a typed doublespaced copy of the Lord's Prayer. Ask the members of each group to work together in writing the Lord's Prayer in their own words in the space at the bottom of the sheet. Ask the group as they write to think of their lives and to add specifics in the places where Jesus made the prayer general. If time allows, the groups can take turns praying their prayers.

4. The next step in the workshop is to provide basic program information. Discuss the program schedule and explain all expectations. Identify any retreats, trips, or other group activities. List these on a sheet of paper and give copies to all persons.

5. The group usually has questions about the program (see Chapter 6). Answer questions at this time, and indicate your willingness to answer other questions that might arise later.

6. Now give the families an opportunity to commit themselves to the vision of this program. If you follow the advice of this book concerning how to assign mentors (see Chapter 3, pages 26-40), then commitment to a specific mentor relationship may come later — after the pastor and design team have confirmed the selection of candidates named earlier by the youth. The vision workshop is, however, an appropriate time to encourage an initial commitment to the program. Close the workshop with a brief worship service, including a prayer for the program and its future participants.

APPENDIX D
Personal Faith Stories

Helping adults and youth with their personal faith stories is an important part of preparing participants for the ministry of mentoring. How do we get in touch with our personal faith story? How can we continue to grow in understanding this story? What are some guidelines to help us decide how to share this story with others?

This appendix contains an exercise that will be helpful in responding to these questions. The exercise can be used in one of two ways. First, it can be used in the one-on-one relationship of mentor and youth. In this setting, the mentor works through the exercise with the friend in faith, which provides an opportunity for the mentoring partners to talk together about their separate and unique faith stories. Second, the exercise can be used in a workshop setting with youth and adults. The material might be incorporated, for example, into the Participant's Workshop agenda in Appendix C.

1. The first step in the awareness of a faith story is to identify possible occasions of communication from God. This seldom entails "handwriting on the wall." Therefore, participants should simply think of the different ways God has communicated with them. Identify the communication event and the date, listing these chronologically on a large sheet of paper. (Most people will have trouble remembering dates.) Participants can also try to divide their lives into time periods. For youth, the periods might include preschool, elementary school, junior high, and (for some) senior high. Adults can list preschool, school, maybe college, and then work by decades after that.

2. Second, participants list events in their lives — both major and minor — that somehow changed who they were. Each person dates these events, lists them on the paper, and identifies the change this event brought about.

3. The next step is to remember strong or gnawing long-term feelings that stirred each person. Was there a time of feeling really good? Was there a time of depression? Was there a time the person felt compelled to do or not to do something? Were there any unidentified feelings? Ask each person to note the time period of these on the chart. Each person then identifies the feeling with what caused it, and what caused it to change. Many will find it difficult to identify or to remember feelings, but encourage them to do their best to complete their lists.

4. The next addition to the chronological list is dreams or visions. God often communicated to biblical persons through dreams and visions. We treat dreams as windows into our deeper self, but we seldom think of them as ways God might communicate with us. We ignore visions or treat them as aberrations. Yet dreams and visions are ways God communicates with those prepared to listen. Encourage participants to think of dreams that affected their lives (including recurring dreams), and add these to their papers.

5. Then each person lists times when no one was around, yet she or he felt a presence nearby. Allow time to add a brief description or identifying phrase to each incident.

6. Finally, each person identifies and writes down times he/she was moved or inspired by a worship experience, musical selection, work of art, speech, sermon, drama, or discussion. By now the paper should be nearly full. If they have room, participants may add other ways that God might come to persons.

7. After everyone finishes writing, each person looks at his or her own paper. Persons can look at their lives in several ways. These could be random happenings dependent only on factors that operate the universe. They could be a combination of universal constants and persons making their own choices. Another possibility is that God is involved in the lives of people and in their responses to various events. The church teaches that God calls us through many events, persons, and feelings. Ask: "Looking at your papers, how would you describe your life if you believe that God has been calling you? What is God trying to say to you as an individual? How do you respond?" Working with these questions can help each individual develop a faith story.

APPENDIX E
A Spiritual Exercise for Mentors

By definition, mentors are persons who are spiritually mature. Indeed, one of the primary characteristics of spiritually mature leaders is that they continue throughout life to reflect on the history, meaning, and pattern of experiences that have shaped them as children of God and followers of Christ so that they may be of help to others on this same journey. The following exercises will help you as a mentor to spend useful time in self-examination and awareness. As a result, more of your own experience of God — both conscious and subconscious — will enter your active awareness. Begin these exercises before your first meeting with your friend in faith, and continue to use them as your relationship develops.

These exercises can also help you and the other leaders of your mentoring program to prepare yourselves for presenting the vision of mentoring to your congregation. Many congregations find it helpful to have laypersons talk about what their faith means to them and why the church is important in their lives. For those churches that have previously had mentoring programs, experienced mentors can discuss the value of the program in their lives. These three-to-five minute talks can be part of the worship service once a week or once a month. These times of sharing and witness help the church think collectively about faith issues.

1. Each day, set aside time to think about your life. Find a block of time while doing laundry, driving to work, or preparing for sleep. Whenever it is, tell yourself to spend all this time on *you*. These days do not have to be in succession. You can skip a day if your schedule does not permit, but try not to miss two days in a row.

2. The first day, think about times in your life when you have been aware of God, but not just those times when you believe God *did* something for you. When did God come into your awareness? When did you think of God's name? When did someone mention the name

of God or an experience with God? When have you called upon God? Begin to think of all these times. Focus on the last year. When were you aware of God in any way? Then focus on the last month. Then focus on today. Then focus on right now. Finally, ask yourself what in your life is the way it is because of your awareness of God. This is a hard question and you may want to think about it for a few days. Ask yourself this question as you go to sleep, knowing you will continue to ponder it the next day.

3. The second day, continue thinking about your awareness of God in your life. Try to push beyond the things you remembered yesterday. Spend more time asking, "What in my life is the way it is because of my awareness of God?"

4. The third day, begin to focus on decisions you make. What helps you make decisions? Do you gather data, mull things over in your head, or ask advice? What enables you to make difficult decisions? Ask yourself if you ever think of God or Christ, or something that you learned in church or in a discussion with other Christians while you are in the decision-making process. Does this awareness help or hinder your decision? At this point don't try to place good or bad tags on your behavior. Accept the way you do things. Don't allow guilt to be present.

5. The fourth day, revisit your awareness of how you make decisions. Ask yourself if any new insights came to you about your decision-making process. Be aware of God's presence as you examine your decision life.

6. The fifth day, think about your prayer life. You probably thought about this the first day as you explored your awareness of God. Examine the times when you formalize a prayer to God. Concentrate on those times when you initiate the prayer rather than times when someone else prays (as in church). What motivates you to pray? Do you pray at special times each day? Are there spontaneous times when you pray?

7. The sixth day, think again about your prayer life. This time concentrate on informal, spontaneous prayers. Are there times when you pray a simple, short prayer in response to something that is happening in your life — something like, "That is beautiful," or "Help me." They must, however, also include at least a vague awareness of God. Remember times in your life when you were in informal prayer. Try to bring these memories right up to the present.

8. On the seventh day, think about your relationships with other people. How does your awareness of God affect your relationships? Does this awareness affect who your friends and associates are? Does this awareness affect how you treat those friends? Do you ever talk to God about your friends? Do you ever talk to your friends about God?

9. On the eighth day, shift your thinking to your acquaintances and to strangers. What does your awareness of God have to do with your relationships with people you do not know very well or at all? By this time you have probably begun to meet with the youth you are to mentor. Continue thinking about your own life. You may begin to spend some of this time thinking about your relationship with the youth in your church.

10. The ninth day, think about how others know you are a Christian. This is not to brag of your achievements. You are, however, called to be a witness to God's work in you. How, without bragging, can you make your witness known to others? Be aware that God is with you helping you with your thoughts today. How can you let God speak through you?

11. The tenth day, think about the following question: "How do people know that God is?" Spend special time today thinking about how you might help your friend in faith with his or her response to this question. Pray and listen to what God is telling you.

12. The next few days, continue thinking about how God is shown through you to others. Try to enhance the natural ways God speaks through you. As you do this, be aware of the times you are with your friend in faith. Show your faith by allowing God to be seen in you. As you spend more and more time with your friend in faith, begin to talk about why you do things. Pay special attention to the silent credit you give God, and try to make more of that public.

13. As the weeks continue, try to maintain some time alone at least a couple of times a week. Think about how your awareness of God has affected your vocation, your personal growth, your leisure, and your work. Keep talking about this with the youth. Let God shine through.

Endnotes

[1]Lewis Carroll, *Alice's Adventures in Wonderland* (New York: Signet Classics, 1964), p. 62.

[2]Homer, *The Odyssey of Homer*, trans. Richard Lattimore (New York: Harper and Row, 1975).

[3]Edward C. Sellner, *Mentoring: The Ministry of Spiritual Kinship* (Notre Dame, Indiana: Ave Marie Press, 1990).

[4]Ibid., pp. 61ff.

[5]*The United Methodist Hymnal* (Nashville, TN: The United Methodist Publishing House, 1989), p. 44.

[6]Ibid.

[7]H. Stephen Glenn, *Creating Capable Young People* (P. O. Box B, Provo, Utah: Quest International/Sunrise Books, 1985). This is a video.

[8]Merton P. Strommen and A. Irene Strommen, *Five Cries of Parents* (Cambridge: Harper and Row, 1985), p. 64.

[9]David Elkind, *All Grown Up and No Place to Go* (Reading, MA: Addison Wesley, 1984), p. 165.

[10]Douglas W. Johnson, *Growing Up Christian in the Twenty-First Century* (Valley Forge, Pennsylvania: Judson Press, 1984), p. 43.

[11]Ellen Rosenberg, *Getting Closer* (New York: Berkeley Books, 1985), p. 201.

[12]Robert N. Bellah et al., *Habits of the Heart* (New York: Harper and Row, 1985), p. 82.

[13]Urie Bronfenbrenner, *Two Worlds of Childhood* (New York: Russell Sage Foundation, 1970), pp. 116-17.

[14]Search Institute, *Effective Christian Education: A National Study of Protestant Congregations* (Minneapolis, Minnesota: Search Institute, 1990).

[15]George H. Gallup, *The Religious Life of Young Americans* (Princeton: The George H. Gallup International Institute, 1992), p. 19.

[16]Search Institute, *Effective Christian Education*, p. 56.

[17]Robert Coles, *Girl Scouts Survey on the Beliefs and Moral Values of America's Children* (New York: Girl Scouts of the United States of America, 1989), p. 2.

[18]William O. Roberts, Jr., *Initiation to Adulthood* (New York: Pilgrim Press, 1982), p. 117.

[19]M. Scott Peck, *The Different Drum: Community Making and Peace* (New York: Simon & Schuster, 1987), pp. 13-15.

[20]William E. Wolfe, *Inviting Youth: A Guide for Adult Leaders of Youth* (Nashville: Discipleship Resources, 1988), p. 55.

[21]Ibid., p. 58.

[22]*The United Methodist Hymnal*, p. 44; and see above pp. 12-13.

[23]James W. Fowler, *Stages of Faith* (San Francisco: Harper and Row, 1981), pp. 98-213; and John H. Westerhoff, *Will Our Children Have Faith?* (New York: Seabury Press, 1976), pp. 89-103.

[24]Search Institute, *Effective Christian Education*, p. 54.

[25]Campbell D. Wycoff, *Religious Education Ministry with Youth* (Birmingham, Alabama: Religious Education Press, 1976), p. 57.

[26]*Webster's Third New International Dictionary* (Springfield, MA: G. & C. Merriam Company, 1966), p. 1412.